NORTHERN I
THE CHOICE

Kevin Boyle and Tom Hadden

PENGUIN BOOKS

PENGUIN BOOKS

Published by the Penguin Group
Penguin Books Ltd, 27 Wrights Lane, London w8 5tz, England
Penguin Books USA Inc., 375 Hudson Street, New York, New York 10014, USA
Penguin Books Australia Ltd, Ringwood, Victoria, Australia
Penguin Books Canada Ltd, 10 Alcorn Avenue, Toronto, Ontario, Canada m4v 3b2
Penguin Books (NZ) Ltd, 182–190 Wairau Road, Auckland 10, New Zealand

Penguin Books Ltd, Registered Offices: Harmondsworth, Middlesex, England

First published 1994
10 9 8 7 6 5 4 3 2 1

Copyright © Kevin Boyle and Tom Hadden, 1994
All rights reserved

The moral right of the authors has been asserted

Set in 10.5/13 pt Monotype Sabon
Typeset by Datix International Limited, Bungay, Suffolk
Printed in England by Clays Ltd, St Ives plc

NORTHERN IRELAND: THE CHOICE

The authors of this book hav̶ ̶

̶o̶r̶t̶h̶e̶r̶n̶ ̶ ̶ ̶ ̶ ̶e̶n̶ ̶

̶ ̶o̶g̶t̶e̶ ̶ ̶ ̶ ̶ ̶ ̶ ̶ ̶ ̶ ̶tly Protes̶ ̶ ̶ ̶ ̶ ̶ t̶o̶ ̶ ̶ ̶ ̶n the north of Co̶u̶. Armagh. He still lives in the townland of Derrybrough̶as a few miles down the River Bann where his ancestors settled three hundred years ago. Kevin Boyle was born and brought up twenty miles further south in Newry, a predominantly Catholic town near the border with the Republic. They met at Cambridge and have worked together since the start of 'the troubles' in 1969. At that time Kevin Boyle was one of the leaders of the civil rights movement; Tom Hadden was the founding editor of *Fortnight*, Northern Ireland's best-known political magazine.

Kevin Boyle worked as a lecturer at Queen's University until 1977 when he was appointed Professor of Law at University College, Galway. In 1986 he moved to London as the founding director of *Article 19*, the international centre against censorship. He is now Professor of Law and Director of the Human Rights Centre at Essex University. He is also visiting professor at University College, Galway, a barrister at law, and legal counsel to the Kurdistan Human Rights Project.

Tom Hadden is now a part-time Professor of Law at Queen's University, Belfast. From 1986 to 1991 he was a member of the Standing Advisory Commission on Human Rights in Northern Ireland and he is currently co-director of a project monitoring states of emergency in divided societies throughout the world. He has written extensively on company law and has been a visiting professor at universities in Canada, Japan and Australia.

Despite these differing paths the authors have continued to work together and have written a number of influential books on Northern Ireland, notably *Ten Years On in Northern Ireland* (1980), *Ireland: A Positive Proposal* (1985) and *The Anglo-Irish Agreement: A Commentary* (1989).

Contents

Figures, Tables and Maps

Figures

Tables

Maps

Rathlin Island

Ballycastle

MOYLE

Coleraine

COLERAINE

Lough Foyle

Ballymoney

BALLYMONEY

Limavady

LIMAVADY

Derry
LONDONDERRY

BALLYMENA
Ballymena

LARNE
Larne

Strabane

STRABANE

MAGHERAFELT
Maghera

ANTRIM

NEWTOWNABBEY
Carrickfergus
Ballyclare · CARRICKFERGUS

Antrim

Belfast Lough

NORTH DOWN
ARDS

COOKSTOWN
Cookstown

Lough Neagh

Belfast
BELFAST

Newtowna

Omagh

OMAGH

Castlereagh
CASTLEREAGH

Dungannon

DUNGANNON

Lurgan
CRAIGAVON

Lisburn
LISBURN

Enniskillen

FERMANAGH

Armagh
ARMAGH

Banbridge
BANBRIDGE

Downpatric

DOWN

NEWRY & MOURNE
Newry

Chronology of Events

1800 Act of Union creates United Kingdom of Great Britain and Ireland

1829 Catholic emancipation

1886 Gladstone's first Home Rule Bill

1893 Gladstone's second Home Rule Bill

1912 Carson mobilizes Ulster Volunteer Force to oppose new Home Rule Bill

1916 Easter rising in Dublin; Irish Republic proclaimed

1918 Last all-Ireland elections

1919 Sinn Féin declares Irish Republic; armed struggle for Irish independence begins

1920 Government of Ireland Act provides for partition of Ireland into a six-county Northern Ireland and a 26-county Southern Ireland, each with its own parliament and government, and for a Council of Ireland to deal with certain matters on an all-Ireland basis

1921 Anglo-Irish Treaty: agreement on the creation of Irish Free State as self-governing dominion and of Northern Ireland as partially self-governing unit within the United Kingdom; Boundary Commission established to review North–South border

1922 Civil war begins between pro-Treaty and anti-Treaty parties in Irish Free State

1923 Pro-Treaty parties win civil war

1925 Report of Boundary Commission suppressed; new Anglo-Irish Treaty confirms six-county area of Northern Ireland and abandons Council of Ireland

1937 New Irish Constitution adopted
1948 Irish Free State becomes a Republic and leaves British Commonwealth
1949 Ireland Act confirms status of Northern Ireland as part of United Kingdom until its Parliament decides otherwise
1956 Abortive IRA campaign in Northern Ireland begins
1962 IRA campaign abandoned
1968 Civil rights campaign begins
1969 British troops deployed in Derry and Belfast
1971 Internment introduced
1972 Northern Ireland Parliament suspended and direct rule introduced
1973 United Kingdom and Republic of Ireland join European Economic Community; new Northern Ireland Constitution; Border poll; elections for Northern Ireland Assembly; Sunningdale Agreement
1974 Power-sharing Northern Ireland Executive established; Ulster Workers Council strike leads to collapse of Executive, dissolution of Assembly and restoration of direct rule
1975 Elections for Northern Ireland Convention; internment phased out
1976 Report of Convention agreed by unionist parties only; Peace People movement launched
1979 First elections for European Parliament held concurrently in Northern Ireland and the Republic of Ireland
1981 Anglo-Irish Intergovernmental Council established at Thatcher–Haughey summit
1982 Elections for Northern Ireland Assembly under Prior's 'rolling devolution' plan; SDLP and Sinn Féin refuse to take up their seats
1983 New Ireland Forum established by main political parties in Republic of Ireland in association with SDLP
1984 New Ireland Forum Report

1985 Anglo-Irish Agreement establishes Anglo-Irish Ministerial Conference and Secretariat to consider Irish government representations on internal government of Northern Ireland; unionist parties withdraw all cooperation with British government

1988 First round of talks between SDLP and Sinn Féin

1989 Official review of Anglo-Irish Agreement confirms established arrangements and promises renewed efforts to seek agreement on devolution for Northern Ireland

1991 Brooke three-strand formula for talks between main Northern Ireland parties and British and Irish governments agreed; internal Strand 1 talks break down after ten weeks

1992 Three-strand talks resumed; Official Unionist delegation meets Irish delegation in Dublin under Strand 2; talks end inconclusively in November; Initiative '92 establishes Opsahl Commission

1993 Opsahl Commission hearings and report; renewed Hume–Adams talks deliver peace proposals to Irish government in September; joint British–Irish Downing Street Declaration in December

Preface

Writing this book has been more than usually difficult. We started work on the project in 1992, at a time when all the parties to the conflict in Northern Ireland seemed to be entrenched in their positions. Little progress was being made in the 'talks process' between the main constitutional parties. The armed struggle was being pursued both by the IRA and by loyalist paramilitaries with increasing rather than diminishing vigour. Our initial idea was to seek a resolution in a European rather than a British–Irish context. But that too became increasingly difficult to sustain in the stand-off over ratification of the Maastricht Treaty of Union. The remaining basis for optimism was the popular involvement in and support for the hearings of the Opsahl Commission and the evidence from opinion polls of widespread support for its final report in June 1993.

Then, in the latter part of 1993 when we had already completed several chapters, events began to move very rapidly. The controversial talks between John Hume and Gerry Adams were brought to an end in September and their proposals for peace were delivered to the Irish government. This was followed by one of the bloodiest periods in the whole conflict with the Shankill Road bomb and Greysteel shootings. Then, in November, it was revealed that the British government had for many months been engaged in a detailed and prolonged 'exchange of views' with representatives of both the IRA and Sinn Féin. Finally, on 15 December, after several high-profile summits, John Major and Albert Reynolds produced what has become known as the Downing Street Declaration. Though this was clearly designed to incorporate the essential elements of the Hume/Adams package which had already been endorsed by the IRA, the IRA made a point of continuing with their campaign of attacks on the security forces and bombs on civilian targets. As we wrote this introduction we were still waiting for any definite response from the republican movement.

Amidst all this confusion we were at times tempted to abandon the book, and to sit back and await whatever outcome might emerge. But we have been persuaded to persevere and to stick more or less to our planned schedule.

One reason is that there are very many people in Ireland and Britain and further afield who are deeply concerned about events in Northern Ireland but who are equally confused by conflicting reports about the situation on the ground, the nature of the conflict and what the peace process may be leading to. For them we have pressed on with our detailed description and analysis of the communal divisions in Northern Ireland, of the continuing conflict which they have produced and of the greatly neglected position of the people in between who want nothing of either. We believe that all those involved in the current peace process need to understand the realities of the situation if they are to pursue policies which will produce a lasting peace and to avoid the dangers of a descent into even greater chaos, of the kind which has been produced in Bosnia.

Another reason is that the path to peace demands a realistic appreciation of the kinds of political and constitutional structures which can help to produce stability in divided societies. We have called them structures for sharing and structures for separation, though, as will be seen, elements of both may perhaps be combined. Even if the 'peace first' strategy proves successful, and the IRA and their loyalist counterparts call off their campaigns and involve themselves in the political process, there will still be a need for agreement on workable political

and constitutional structures. Whatever happens, all those involved in the political talks that must eventually take centre
stage will have to make difficult choices between the various
available structures. We hope that our analysis will assist
them.

A final reason is that, ultimately, it is for the people in
Northern Ireland and in the Republic to make a choice as to
how they are to live in the island of Ireland, whether it be
separately or together. A settlement which does not command
the support of a substantial number of people in both communities in Northern Ireland will not stick. And there is a real
choice to be made between a settlement which involves greater
sharing and one which involves greater separation. We believe
that all the people of Northern Ireland and of the Republic of
Ireland should be directly involved in making that choice. In
the final chapter of this book we have suggested some ways in
which that might be done.

Our thanks are as usual owed to the many people who have
helped us in developing our ideas and in producing this book.
Those who are directly involved in the political and governmental processes will not wish to be identified. Among our
academic colleagues special thanks are due to Fred Boal, Brice
Dickson, Sydney Elliott, Mari Fitzduff, Graham Gudgin, Colin
Irwin, Liam Kennedy and Jim Mostinckx. Thanks, too, are
due to the Nuffield Foundation for providing initial support
for our work in 1992 on European dimensions to the Northern
Ireland problem, to the Joseph Rowntree Reform Trust for assistance with the costs of working together at a distance of more
than five hundred miles and to the Controller of Her Majesty's
Stationery Office for permission to make use of unpublished
census data. Miranda McAllister, Penelope Dunn and Peter
Carson of Penguin Books have provided invaluable editorial
advice and assistance, not least in keeping us to our schedules
and getting the book out so quickly. And our families have as

usual not only had to put up with our numerous absences but have made their own contributions: Joan and Chris by curtailing our wilder flights of fantasy, Rachel and Ellen by working on tables and charts, and Mark, Stephen and JP by helping with printing and making space on our respective computers.

T.H.   K.B.
                                                                                    25 February 1994

PART I

THE BASIC CHOICE

Can the current search for peace in Northern Ireland succeed? If it fails, could Northern Ireland become another Bosnia? Have the twenty-five years of relatively restrained communal conflict in Northern Ireland to date been merely a prelude to a full-scale civil war and a thoroughgoing ethnic separation? Or can the two communities there be persuaded to settle their differences and live together in peace? Can the British and Irish governments develop the Anglo-Irish Agreement of 1985 and the Joint Declaration of December 1993 into a new deal which actually delivers peace and stability, or could they be trapped by their internal political concerns into supporting incompatible and undeliverable demands by those who claim to represent the Protestant and Catholic communities in Northern Ireland? And do these communal leaders – whether political or paramilitary – really represent a majority in either community? Or are the ordinary people of Northern Ireland being led by the nose by their political leaders and warlords into an ever-increasing communal separation which most of them don't want, as some argue has happened already in what was Yugoslavia? And if so, what should be done about it? How can the ordinary people in Northern Ireland be given a democratic choice between conflict and compromise, between separation and sharing? Is there any way in which the ordinary people in Britain and the Republic of Ireland can help, or must they suffer the damage and destruction caused by Irish terrorism indefinitely?

The aim of this book it to provide answers to questions like these. Some of the answers may be unpalatable. But events in what was Yugoslavia have shown that unpalatable answers may sometimes be unavoidable. Some answers may seem, at first sight, to be inappropriate in the sense that many of those interested in Northern Ireland would prefer other questions to have been given greater prominence, not least the question of Irish unification. Others may seem to be unhelpful in the sense that they will depend on answers to yet more questions or leave open the possibility of several different answers, depending on what politicians and people in Northern Ireland and elsewhere choose – or allow to be chosen for them. That at least should not be unwelcome. One of the most important conclusions of this book will be that there are real choices to be made: if the right questions are asked and appropriate answers are given we can all be spared the anguish of another Bosnia, but if the wrong questions are asked or the wrong answers are given there is a real risk of the situation deteriorating as quickly and disastrously as it did in former Yugoslavia.

Any comparison of this kind between Northern Ireland and Bosnia – or any other troublespot – must obviously be treated with some caution. Every ethnic or communal conflict is unique. But what has happened in Kosava, Croatia and Bosnia may help to remind us of the terrifying force which sentiments of national or communal identity may generate, and that one of the fundamental choices that arises in most conflicts of this kind is between separation or sharing: whether the different communities can go on living together and sharing their facilities and their structures for government or whether their differences can be accommodated only by living apart. Living together does not, of course, rule out all forms of separate provision. Distinctive communities, like those in Belgium, may agree to maintain separate educational systems and separate social facilities without conflict. And separation may take many forms – from residential and social segregation to the development of separate systems of local self-government and ultimately complete territorial and constitutional separation.

But there is a clear choice to be made between policies based on the acceptance of separation and policies based on the objective of sharing.

In Northern Ireland the forces of communal separation have been at work throughout the 'troubles' and have already produced a high degree of residential segregation. More than half the people in many areas of Northern Ireland (as will be shown in greater detail in Part II) now live in districts or estates which are more than 90 per cent communally 'pure'. But official government policy in almost every sphere is still committed to the objective of greater integration and sharing between members of the two communities, not least in the sharing of governmental power and in employment. The question posed by experience elsewhere is whether that policy is right and whether workable structures for sharing can be put in place. Or would it be more realistic to accept that the forces of communal separation are irresistible and that official policy should be altered accordingly to provide for a deliberate move towards developing structures for separation?

CHAPTER 1

Separation or Sharing

What this fundamental choice between separation and sharing is likely to involve must be fully understood before any sensible decisions can be made. One way of explaining is to give a simple picture of what the result might be if either separation or sharing was to be systematically and effectively pursued – or allowed to happen by default – and to sketch some of the ways in which these distinctive futures might actually be brought about.

The communal separation option

The choice of communal separation as an acceptable objective would clearly involve a continuation of the trend towards residential segregation that has been taking place since the start of the present troubles in 1969. This has been most observable in the bigger towns. As a result of mass intimidation in the early 1970s[1] and a slower process of both forced and voluntary movement since, the Catholic population in Belfast is now, as shown in Table 1.1a, heavily concentrated in West Belfast and a few other well-defined areas – Ardoyne, the Markets, Lower Ormeau, Short Strand. The latest census figures also show a parallel reduction in the proportion of Catholics in some Protestant areas in the Greater Belfast area. In the City of London/Derry similar pressures have resulted in a huge decline in the number of Protestants on the west bank of the River Foyle, as shown in Table 1.1b. This pattern has been

Table 1.1 *Population movement in parts of Belfast, London/Derry and two rural areas between 1971 and 1991*

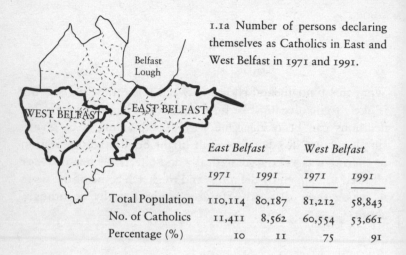

1.1a Number of persons declaring themselves as Catholics in East and West Belfast in 1971 and 1991.

	East Belfast		West Belfast	
	1971	1991	1971	1991
Total Population	110,114	80,187	81,212	58,843
No. of Catholics	11,411	8,562	60,554	53,661
Percentage (%)	10	11	75	91

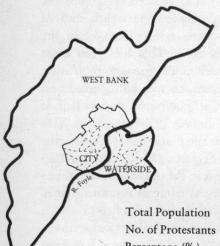

1.1b Number of persons declaring themselves as Protestants on the East and West Banks of the Foyle in the London/Derry area.

	Waterside		West Bank + City	
	1971	1991	1971	1991
Total Population	19,220	18,154	48,083	55,901
No. of Protestants	10,952	10,806	9,844	2,586
Percentage (%)	57	59	20	5

1.1c Number of persons declaring themselves as Protestants in South Armagh (9 Wards) and in the Castlederg area (2 Wards) in 1971 and 1991.

	South Armagh		Castlederg area	
	1971	1991	1971	1991
Total Population	20,507	23,605	2,599	2,912
No. of Protestants	3,118	2,749	1,968	1,928
Percentage (%)	15	12	76	66

Crown copyright 1971 and 1992. Published by permission of the Controller of Her Majesty's Stationery Office.

replicated in other towns throughout Northern Ireland, most of which now have clearly defined areas in which the minority population – of Catholics in the east and of Protestants in the west – cluster together for mutual support and a feeling of safety. The trend in rural areas is less stark. Some unionist politicians have repeatedly alleged that the IRA has been deliberately targeting isolated Protestant families and farms in border areas in pursuit of what would now be called 'ethnic cleansing'. But the evidence from census figures, as indicated in Table 1.1c, is that Protestant numbers in border areas have declined only marginally and that the major change has been a rapid increase in the numbers of Catholics. The conclusion must be that in urban areas the two communities are moving into what they regard as safer areas, while in rural areas they are staying put on their land.

This more or less spontaneous population movement – though it has often been traumatic for those involved – has increased the extent to which most members of the two communities can avoid any serious discussion of their differences. They have always gone to separate schools. They play and watch separate sports. They tend to patronize their own shops and to go to their own doctors, dentists and solicitors. And despite the efforts of the Fair Employment Commission, as will be seen, many places of work are effectively segregated. If the two communities are already choosing to live apart, why should they not be allowed or even encouraged to complete the process if that would ensure peace and a stable future for both?

It would certainly not be difficult to develop policies which would recognize and facilitate communal separation. One possibility would be the development of separate agencies to provide public services to members of the two communities. There are already some examples. A publicly funded Catholic Maintained Schools Council has recently been created on a statutory basis to manage the separate Catholic schools sector. This has led to corresponding demands from some Protestant churches for the creation of an equivalent Protestant Schools Council to replace or supplement the work of the cross-communal and broadly representative Education and Library Area Boards. Further development along these lines might result in the creation of a wider range of separate publicly funded communal bodies to support and control separate cultural and sporting facilities. Separate structures for policing in predominantly Catholic or Protestant areas might also be created to supplement or replace the theoretically cross-communal but largely Protestant Royal Ulster Constabulary. There is already some pressure for this on the twin grounds that the RUC is unacceptable in many nationalist areas and cannot therefore provide proper policing and that the recruitment of an officially recognized Catholic policing service would help to diminish the influence of para-militaries and to create employment in Catholic areas.[2] The pursuit of these policies might in turn lead to the creation of

multi-purpose communal bodies elected on a district or cantonal basis to administer all those facilities and services which
were allocated on a communal rather than a cross-communal
basis. The objective would be to give to members of each
community effective control over their own affairs and to
minimize the need for cooperation and compromise between
them.

Formal structures for separate communal autonomy are
well established in some other divided societies. There are
elected or representative communal bodies in Belgium, Canada
and Switzerland whose function it is to look after the interests
of or provide services for members of a single linguistic or
religious community. Some of these structures for communal
separation, whether on a territorial or a functional basis, are
clearly workable and have provided a measure of stability
where they have been adopted, as will be shown in greater
detail in Chapter 7. The more difficult question is whether any
such structures could be sustained in the particular circumstances of Northern Ireland. There may be a greater danger
that the development of such structures would lead to the
break up of Northern Ireland. Further residential segregation
and separate communal government might ultimately lead to a
formal repartition under which a smaller and more exclusively
Protestant state of Northern Ireland would be established, thus
permitting the rest of its existing territory to be absorbed into
the Republic of Ireland. There are some arguments in favour of a
deliberate repartition of this kind. Maps of some possible
boundaries have already been produced, as shown in Map 1.1.

There are also strong arguments against any such policy.
There would clearly be a risk that, without a substantial
movement of population from Catholic enclaves in the new
Northern Ireland, any repartition would merely perpetuate the
underlying problem on a slightly reduced scale. But voluntary
population movement could be encouraged. Government grants
could be offered for movement to appropriate areas or for the

Map 1.1 *Some possible repartitions*

British Ulster

Irish Ulster

This option maximizes the area of 'British Ulster' while providing for West Belfast to be part of 'Irish Ulster'; on 1981 figures it would have resulted in a minority of some 20% of Catholics in 'British Ulster' and some 16% of Protestants in 'Irish Ulster'.	This option maximizes the area of 'Irish Ulster' but leaves West Belfast in 'British Ulster'; on 1981 figures it would have resulted in a minority of some 26% of Catholics in 'British Ulster' and some 21% of Protestants in 'Irish Ulster'.

Source: Liam Kennedy, *The Two Ulsters*, 1986

exchange of houses or farms. Policies of this kind have been adopted in many decolonization operations and in the aftermath of some ethnic conflicts. White settlers in what was Rhodesia were offered compensation for giving up their land when Zimbabwe was granted its independence in the 1960s. More than two million Greeks and Turks were persuaded to move into the newly defined boundaries of Greece and Turkey in a coordinated operation in the aftermath of the Aegean war of 1922–3.

Whatever the longer-term merits of greater communal separation – which will be discussed at length in Part III of this book – there can be little doubt that it would be relatively easy to bring about. The simplest and most abrupt method would be a unilateral decision by the British government to withdraw from Northern Ireland. That would be a signal for the mobilization of paramilitary forces on either side. The barricades and no-go areas that were so prominent a feature in some areas of Belfast and Derry in the early days of the troubles from 1969 to 1971 would reappear and there would be a nasty competition for control over territory by the respective warlords on either side. The extent of this would depend largely on the stance of the RUC and the locally recruited soldiers in what used to be known as the Ulster Defence Regiment – now the Royal Irish Regiment – and of the Irish Army. It took a massive show of strength by the British Army in Operation Motorman in 1972 to dismantle the defences of 'Free Derry' and other such enclaves. It is doubtful whether the RUC on its own would have the strength or the equipment to carry out a similar operation, even if they wished to. It is more likely that they would seek to contain the situation by accepting *de facto* control by the IRA and the UDA in their respective territories and by seeking to maintain a measure of normality elsewhere. It is also unlikely that the Irish Defence Forces would want to intervene in areas under the *de facto* control of the RUC or to move into areas under loyalist control except in the case of small enclaves in otherwise nationalist zones. In any event, there would be a large flow of refugees as ordinary people in both communities and from the in-betweens sought to get on the right side of the emerging territorial boundaries or to escape to Britain or the Republic. The result would not be unlike that in some parts of Bosnia, though the scale of weaponry on either side would be unlikely to be so destructive.

A precipitate and unilateral British withdrawal of this kind is unlikely, though it would not be without precedent. It is more or less what the British government decided on in Palestine in 1945, leaving the Palestinians and the Jews to fight it out for control over territory – a conflict that has yet to be finally resolved. It is more likely that some attempt would be made either to hand over control of Northern Ireland to the Republic without the consent of the unionist majority or else to establish a representative government and an organized security force effectively controlled by Protestants. But the end result might not be very different. Loyalist paramilitaries and the bulk both of the Protestant community and perhaps also of the RUC would certainly resist any attempt by either British or Irish forces to impose Irish unification; the resulting conflict would produce the same pressure for population movement as a simple British withdrawal. An attempt to hand over control to a purely Protestant government would be likely to meet with a corresponding upsurge in paramilitary activity on the Catholic side with similar results. In the absence of some measure of agreement on shared structures for government, or on a workable allocation of territory between the two communities or between the Protestants and the Irish government, it is hard to see how British withdrawal on any terms could be achieved without a significant escalation of internal conflict and the communal separation that would come with it.

Greater communal separation might also be brought about more gradually by deliberate governmental action or by default. The adoption of measures like those outlined above to provide for greater autonomy for members of the two main communities might prove to be sufficiently acceptable to permit a return to peace and stability. But they might equally lead to an acceleration of the kind of population movement which would pave the way for eventual repartition. So too, of course, would measures to facilitate relocation with a view to creating more communally homogeneous units for local government. Even the present system of direct rule could in time produce the same result. Direct rule is designed to be temporary, pending some unspecified future constitutional settlement. The lack of any democratic base and the continuation of terrorist activity, if the present peace process fails, may in the longer term

generate sufficient population movement over time to make
formal separation or repartition the only practicable solution.

The communal sharing option

The alternative option of communal sharing is one in which
Northern Ireland would continue as a unit of government
within which every effort is made to encourage cooperation
between the two communities and to maintain institutions in
which representatives of each can share power and responsibility. This is the current policy of the British government. It is
built into the Anglo-Irish Agreement of 1985. And it remains
the objective of both the British and Irish governments in the
continuing 'talks' or 'peace' process, although it is not empha-
sized in the Joint Declaration of December 1993.

The central plank of this approach is the search for agreement between the main constitutional parties – those which do
not support or condone violence – on a system of government
for Northern Ireland in which representatives of both communities can agree to participate. That will almost certainly involve
the development of institutions for cooperation between Northern Ireland and the Republic of Ireland. But it will also involve a
wider range of policies and agencies designed to encourage
greater cooperation and integration between the two communities within Northern Ireland.

One of the most important of the government's current
policies in this sphere is the attempt to ensure that all major
employers, both public and private, maintain a fair balance of
Protestants and Catholics in their workforce. Though the fair
employment legislation was introduced primarily to eliminate
all forms of discrimination in employment, its practical implementation now involves strict monitoring by the Fair Employment Commission of the proportion of Protestants and Catholics in most places of employment and thus has the effect of

requiring the integration of the two communities in this sphere. The government has also sought to encourage the development of contacts between the two communities in education through the element in the new Northern Ireland Curriculum known as Education for Mutual Understanding, and more generally by funding inter-communal initiatives and activities through the Community Relations Council. It has also committed itself to supporting and funding the development of new integrated schools where there is sufficient demand, though without giving much real priority to them.[3]

There is clearly scope for the further development of policies of this kind. Additional powers could be given to local district councils which practise power-sharing between representatives of the two communities. More resources and incentives could be offered to the development of integrated schools as a major means of encouraging positive contacts between the two communities, as opposed to the prevailing current objective of ensuring strictly equal treatment for two separate school systems. Similar incentives could be provided for those who wish to live together in integrated housing estates, both in the public and private sectors, as a means of halting or reversing the trend towards residential segregation. The objective of these policies, it should be stressed, would be to achieve greater mutual recognition and cooperation between the two major communities in Northern Ireland rather than assimilation of one by the other.

Building effective structures for shared government would enable the people of Northern Ireland to face confidently questions about their longer-term future. Northern Ireland might continue indefinitely as a separate unit of government within the United Kingdom with agreed provisions for cooperation with the Republic of Ireland. The people of Northern Ireland might seek to develop this cooperation into some form of joint or shared status within both the United Kingdom and the Republic of Ireland. Alternatively, they might at some time seek acceptance within the European Union as a special regional unit in which both the British and Irish governments had legitimate responsibilities. Agreement might equally be reached on the unification of Ireland under a federal or confederal constitution which made special provision for the continued shared government of Northern Ireland by representatives of both major communities. But the underlying basis of any of these arrangements would be the indefinite continuation of special measures to protect the interests of both major communities whose members would continue to share responsibility for their own government without any major movements of population.

The way in which these various objectives might be achieved will form a major part of the discussion in Part III. The British and Irish governments together might develop the current 'peace process' into a more effective and successful round of all-party talks, in which Sinn Féin and other representatives of the paramilitaries might be involved. The two governments might also seek to develop and impose their own proposals in default of agreement by the main Northern Ireland parties. Use might also be made of what may be called a referendum strategy, explained in Chapter 8, to establish whether there is sufficient popular support in both communities for the option of communal sharing rather than communal separation. For the moment, it is sufficient to state that greater communal sharing is unlikely to be achieved by the indefinite continuation of the current political impasse or by default. That is much more likely, as suggested above, to lead to greater communal separation.

The challenge to Britain, Ireland and Europe

If the real choice over Northern Ireland is between separation or sharing for the people there, why should anyone else in Britain, Ireland or Europe be concerned? Why should people in

Northern Ireland not be left to sort out their own future for themselves in their own time?

One reason is the likelihood that, while the question remains undecided, IRA terrorism in Britain and Europe and the threat of loyalist terrorism in the Republic of Ireland will continue. So, too, will the fatalities, anguish and inconvenience which they cause, and the payment for damage and destruction and the preventive security measures which they make necessary. The IRA has learned that shootings and bombings in Britain and Europe pay higher dividends than their equivalent in Northern Ireland. That message is unlikely to be ignored by their loyalist counterparts if the need should arise to take their struggle to a wider public. The cost of a single bomb in London to the UK insurance market can be as high as £1 billion. The cost of maintaining British troops at their present level in Northern Ireland is around £300 million per year. The cost of their security measures to the Irish government is around IR£200 million per year, a much higher proportion of their available resources.

Another reason is that everyone in Britain, Ireland and Europe has an interest in the peaceful resolution of the nationalist, ethnic and communal conflicts that have re-emerged in the 1990s. Serious ethnic conflict anywhere in Europe has the capacity to set at naught the hope for greater European integration and prosperity. It is all very well to say that the parties to internal conflicts should be left to fight it out among themselves. The reality is that, if any such conflict is allowed to fester and escalate and eventually reach the level of intensity of that in the Balkans, other states inevitably become involved. Television pictures of the victims of a serious escalation of the conflict in Northern Ireland would make inaction politically impossible and the flow of refugees, though not as large as that from Croatia and Bosnia, would not be inconsiderable. There would inevitably be demands for the deployment of European or United Nations peacekeeping forces.

There must also be broader concerns over issues of pluralism and democracy. Almost every country in Europe has its minorities which have been created by the process of drawing hard and fast political boundaries between sovereign states. In many cases these minorities have been peacefully absorbed into the wider national community or allowed to retain their separate identity with a measure of local autonomy. In some, however, the strains between two or more communities which have been locked together in a single state have led to ever-increasing problems over demands for separate provision and separate facilities and ultimately for self-determination. In such cases there are two broad options. Other countries and the international community may join together to work towards a peaceful settlement in which the problems created by history and by the drawing of rigid boundaries can be resolved by international cooperation. This may involve the development of structures for sharing, as in Holland or the German-speaking region of Italy, known as Alto-Adige. Or it may involve the development of structures for communal separation, as in Belgium. Or they may stand aside and allow the situation to fester until it erupts into either a forced repartition like that in Cyprus or the shameful sacrifice of a multi-ethnic state as in Bosnia. To stand aside from the problems in Northern Ireland and, in effect, to allow its future to be resolved by force of arms would be a denial of the new European commitment to democracy within the Conference for Security and Cooperation in Europe and the European Union.[4] What happens in a place like Northern Ireland, where the problems of history, of disputes over frontiers and of communal separation or sharing are posed with particular starkness, is of concern to us all.

PART II

TAKING STOCK

It is all too easy to make a case – or a TV programme – for one of the major policy options for Northern Ireland by giving a few well-chosen facts and figures. A persuasive case for withdrawing British troops and working towards Irish unification can be based on the long history of failed campaigns by the British Army in Ireland and the continuing series of human rights abuses which have been committed by British soldiers during the current conflict in Northern Ireland. A persuasive case for working towards some form of communal separation or repartition as the only way of achieving lasting peace and stability can, as shown in Part I, be based on the recent trend towards increasing physical separation between the two communities. A persuasive case for continuing with the current inter-governmental policy of encouraging sharing between the two communities can likewise be based on opinion-poll evidence of the expressed wishes of representative samples of voters.

That kind of presentation is not a satisfactory way of making decisions in the real world. Difficult political decisions usually require a careful balancing of conflicting considerations. The purpose of the chapters which follow in this Part is to take stock of the situation in Northern Ireland, and of Northern Ireland's place in the United Kingdom, in the island of Ireland, and in Europe as fully and objectively as can be managed without reference to any particular proposal for action. That will involve attempting to answer a different and more general set of questions. Are there really just two communities in Northern Ireland? And what about the people who don't belong or don't want to belong to either? What is the impact of terrorism on attitudes and practical policies in Northern Ireland? And what is the relevance of recent developments in Europe to possible resolutions of the Northern Ireland problem?

CHAPTER 2

The Two Communities and the People in Between

Everyone accepts that there are two communities in Northern Ireland. People in Northern Ireland are certainly used to thinking about and responding to every aspect of the problem in terms of the numbers or proportions of Protestants and Catholics. Most opinion polls are conducted on that basis. There is continuing interest in the precise balance between the Protestant and Catholic communities and likely future trends. There is continuing concern over communal differentials in employment and unemployment and related differences in household income and general prosperity. There is also a high degree of social separation between them. Segregation in the educational and sporting spheres is well established. And members of both communities tend to patronize their own shops, their own doctors, dentists and solicitors and other services. The trend towards increasing residential segregation which has already been described is clearly adding to these tendencies.

Almost everyone also accepts that the essence of the Northern Ireland problem lies in the conflict between the two communities. This is now the dominant view among political and social scientists.[1] Inter-communal conflict has been rediscovered and is the focus of academic and political attention throughout the world. Only the Provisional IRA, Sinn Féin and their supporters cling to the view that it is the continuing British colonial involvement in Northern Ireland that is causing the conflict, that once the British link is removed peace and stability will automatically follow.[2]

And yet there must be some caution about the wholesale

acceptance of a simple two-communities analysis. One indication of the problem is the lack of agreement as to what they
should be called.[3] The terms Protestant and Catholic, unionist
and nationalist, and loyalist and republican are all used. Yet
they all have slightly different shades of meaning. Protestant
and Catholic are the simplest labels, though some people
dislike using them because they imply that the dispute is
primarily religious, which is misleading. The most frequent
alternatives are unionist and nationalist. But that too can be
misleading. Almost all Protestants are unionist in the sense of
wanting to retain the link with Britain. Only a very few are
willing to follow in the footsteps of the historic Protestant
leaders of Irish independence like Wolfe Tone and Douglas
Hyde. Again, not all Catholics are nationalist in the sense of
wishing to join with the Republic of Ireland. And yet unionist
Catholics would not regard themselves as being part of the
Protestant unionist community. The terms loyalist and republican are even less satisfactory, since they are normally used to
refer to members of one or other community with uncompromising political views and a tendency to use or accept the use
of violence in the pursuit of their objectives. Only a minority in
either community can properly be called loyalists and
republicans.

These doubts over what to call the two communities point
to another more serious problem: what the conflict between
them is about. Is it primarily constitutional – a dispute between
unionists and nationalists over the status of Northern Ireland?
Or is it primarily about political power or economic domination or control of land – a struggle by the Protestants to
maintain their dominant position and by the Catholics to
overturn it? And is there really no purely religious dimension?
And what of those who do not wish to subscribe to the
prevailing ethos in either community or to be regarded as
belonging to either? One of the major criticisms of the two-
communities approach is that it may exaggerate and accentuate

the degree of division and separation. The compilation of statistics on any aspect of the conflict typically involves allocating as many individuals or households as possible to either the Protestant or the Catholic community. Mixed households arising from mixed marriages, households and individuals who reject any exclusive communal affiliation and those who have moved to Northern Ireland from Britain or further afield are therefore ignored or eliminated from the analysis. Though there is little hard statistical evidence on many of these matters, there can be little doubt that there is, and always has been, much more intermingling between the two communities than the communal separation theory suggests. On some issues, such as integrated education and certain political proposals, as will be seen, there is evidence which suggests that more people favour increased cooperation and sharing rather than further separation.

All this suggests that the two communities are less monolithic and mutually exclusive than the communal conflict analysis suggests, and that there is a substantial body of people who fall somewhere in between on some or all of the matters on which the two communities are divided. The two communities certainly exist. But their composition is flexible and variable and there is a significant third community in between. The purpose of this chapter is to take stock of the extent to which the two main communities and those who fall in between can be identified, and to describe the degree of communal coherence, separation and intermingling in a number of major spheres: the distribution of population and likely future trends; the extent of residential segregation and intermingling; the degree of social separation and intermingling in education, leisure activities and culture; the relative economic prosperity of members of the two communities and others; current patterns of voting and of party support; and, finally, the evidence from opinion polls as to the attitudes and aspirations of all the people of Northern Ireland rather than merely those who can most easily be allocated to one or other community.

Communal population distribution

The current distribution of Protestants and Catholics in Northern Ireland can be directly related to the settlement patterns of the seventeenth century, as illustrated in Map 2.1. In the early part of that period large parts of the two eastern counties of Antrim and Down, which appear to have been thinly populated at the time, were settled by lowland Scottish Presbyterians in a number of semi-official plantations. The north coast of Antrim is very close to Scotland and there had always been a flow of people from one to the other. All but one of the other counties in the province of Ulster – Armagh, Londonderry, Tyrone, Fermanagh, Donegal, and Cavan – were the subject of an officially organized plantation following the defeat of the O'Neill rebellion at the turn of the seventeenth century and the 'flight of the earls' in 1607. But in these counties the settlement was less complete and large numbers of the established Irish population were included in the new grants of land by the 'undertakers' who carried out the operation on behalf of the English king. The settlers, most of whom came from the North of England, also acquired large tracts of land in the remaining county of Monaghan. The incoming Protestants naturally chose the best land and the Catholics were granted or remained on land in the less fertile and more mountainous areas.

The result was that Protestants became an overwhelming majority of the population in most of Antrim and Down, excluding the Mountains of Mourne and the Glens of Antrim, and formed a clear majority in the north of County Armagh, the east of County Londonderry and in some parts of the counties of Tyrone and Fermanagh. But in many western and southern areas, particularly in the counties of Donegal, Cavan and Monaghan, the incoming Protestants never formed more than a substantial minority.

During the nineteenth century there was further population

Official plantation

Unofficial plantation

Donegal

Londonderry

Antrim

ULSTER

Tyrone

Fermanagh

Armagh

Down

Monaghan

Cavan

CONNAUGHT

LEINSTER

MUNSTER

Map 2.1 *The pattern of plantation in Ulster in the seventeenth century*

movement as large numbers of Catholics from rural areas moved into Belfast and other smaller industrial towns in the eastern part of Ulster in search of work in the new linen and textile factories. In Belfast, the incoming Catholics tended to congregate in well-defined areas close to the main railway stations and there were repeated sectarian disturbances in the latter part of the century.[4] As a result, there is a substantial minority of Catholics in all the major industrial towns, even in areas which had hitherto been predominantly Protestant.

This pattern of settlement both in the country and the towns, it should be noted, differed substantially from that in the rest of Ireland, where incoming Protestant landlords and the professional classes tended to be superimposed on the pre-existing Catholic peasantry and were always heavily outnumbered by them.

The current distribution on a district council basis as recorded in the 1991 census is illustrated in Map 2.3. It shows clearly how the proportion of Protestants declines from an overwhelming majority of around 90 per cent in some of the districts around Belfast to a clear majority of from 55 per cent to 75 per cent in Belfast and the central districts of Coleraine, Ballymoney, Ballymena, Larne, Antrim, Lisburn, Craigavon and Armagh. In the remainder of the western and southern districts adjacent to the Irish Republic and in Moyle, Magherafelt and Cookstown there is a clear, and in some parts a substantial, majority of Catholics. In every area, however, there is a significant minority of people who either refused to state their religion or stated that they had none. The figures for these two groups are remarkably constant at around 7 per cent of non-stated and 4 per cent of no religion in most of the 26 districts, as is also shown in Map 2.3.

Many analyses of the current balance between the two communities have attempted to resolve the difficulty caused by refusals to state religion – which was particularly significant in the 1981 census due to a political boycott in some nationalist areas – by various methods of allocating the 'did not state' or

1926

1961

Map 2.2 *Catholic population by county in 1926 and 1961*

even the 'no religion' category to one or other main community. This presentation of the census results clearly increases the apparent proportion of both Catholics and Protestants and further highlights the extent of the communal division. It is usually justified on the grounds that some people prefer not to state their religion because they live in an area dominated by the 'other side' and want to keep a low profile. It is equally likely, however, that most of those people who refused to state their religion or said they had none did so because they did not want to be classified in that way and that they should instead be treated as a distinctive group which falls between the two main communities. This group almost certainly includes a number of people who have moved into Northern Ireland from Britain or further afield. Another major section is likely to be the partners or children of the increasing number of mixed marriages. It has been estimated that up to one-fifth of all marriages in the Belfast area now involve a Catholic and a Protestant partner.[5] Many of these deliberately choose integrated schooling for their children as a positive assertion of their ties to both rather than a single community. It seems wrong, whether for the purposes of assessing the balance between the two communities or for fair employment monitoring, to insist on allocating them to one or other major community rather than to a separate non-communal or inter-communal group in their own right. The size of this group cannot, of course, be accurately assessed merely from the census figures; it is arguable that it is much larger than the census figures for 'refused to state' or 'no religion'. But even if the presentation in Map 2.3 is inaccurate, it at least has the advantage of drawing attention to the existence of a significant body of people in between the two main communal groups.

Map 2.3 *Proportions of Catholics, Protestants and people in between (no religion or not stated) in the 26 District Council areas in 1971 and 1991*

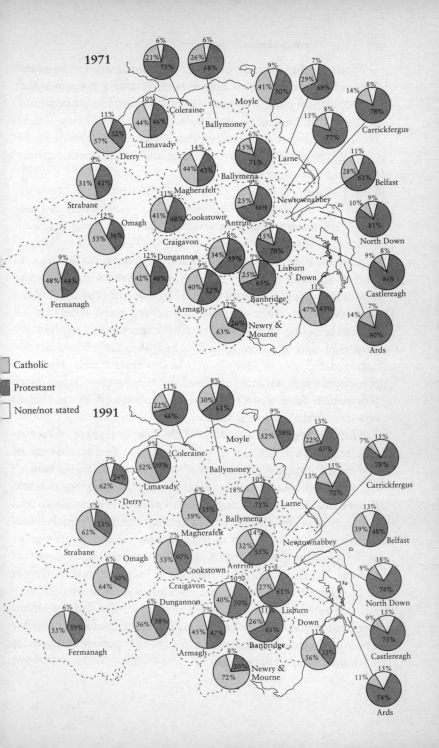

1971

6%
21% 73%

6%
26% 68%

9%
41% 50%

7%
29% 69%

14%
8%
78%
Carrickfergus

10%
Coleraine

Moyle

Ballymoney

11%
57% 32%
Limavady

15%
8%
77%

9%
51% 41%
Derry

14%
44% 43%
Magherafelt

6%
15%
71%
Ballymena

Larne

11%
28% 61%
Belfast

Strabane

11%
41% 48%
Cookstown

9%
25% 66%
Newtownabbey

10%
9%
81%
North Down

12%
53% 36%
Omagh

Antrim

7%

9%
9%
9%
9%
84%
Castlereagh

9%
48% 44%
Fermanagh

12% Dungannon
42% 46%

8%
34% 59%
Craigavon

15%
78%
Lisburn

Down

7%
80%
Ards

9%
40% 52%
Armagh

7%
25% 65%
Banbridge

11%
47% 43%

12%
26%
63%
Newry &
Mourne

Catholic

Protestant

None/not stated **1991**

11%
22% 66%

8%
30% 61%

9%
52% 39%

13%
22% 65%

7%
15%
78%
Carrickfergus

9%
Coleraine

Moyle

Ballymoney

7%
52% 39%
24%
62%
Limavady

13%
15%
72%

5%
62% 33%
Derry

6%
59% 35%
Magherafelt

18%
71%
Ballymena

Larne

10%

13%
39% 48%
Belfast

Strabane

7%
53% 40%
Cookstown

14%
32% 55%
Newtownabbey

18%
9%
74%
North Down

6%
64% 30%
Omagh

Antrim

12%

10%

9%
15%
75%
Castlereagh

6%
55% 39%
Fermanagh

6% Dungannon
56% 38%

7%
40% 50%
Craigavon

27% 61%
Lisburn

Down

11%
74%
Ards

7%
45% 47%
Armagh

11%
26% 61%
Banbridge

11%
56% 33%

8%
20%
72%
Newry &
Mourne

Whatever the size of this inter-communal group, however, the overall picture is of a classic ethnic frontier zone in which the population closest to one adjacent territory – Scotland and the North of England – gradually changes from being almost exclusively of that nationality or culture to being almost exclusively of the nationality or culture of another adjacent territory – the Republic of Ireland.[6]

Communal population trends

It must also be remembered that the population balance in frontier zones of this kind is rarely static. Events in Bosnia and other areas of ethnic conflict are a reminder of how quickly the situation may change. A snapshot at any given time can tell only part of the story. It is equally important to explain the nature of and reasons for any changes which have already occurred and also to identify any likely future trends. How has the population balance changed in the seventy years since Northern Ireland was created as a separate unit in 1921? And how may it change in the future?

The most significant feature of the first fifty years of Northern Ireland as a distinctive unit was probably the absence of any major change. There was some population movement in the period of the initial 'troubles' from 1918 to 1923. Some Protestants moved from the counties of Monaghan, Cavan and Donegal into Fermanagh and other parts of Northern Ireland. Whether this was a result of intimidation or of disappointment at having been 'abandoned' by the unionist leaders is not known. But the population balance in each of the six counties of Northern Ireland between 1926 and 1961, as shown in Map 2.2, remained remarkably stable despite a substantially higher birthrate in the Catholic community. The explanation for this lies in differential emigration rates. In this period many more Catholics emigrated to Britain and further afield, not least because it was more difficult for them to find jobs. It was one of the less well-publicized but widely understood objectives – and achievements – of the unionist regime to ensure that 'their people' were able to find jobs at home in preference to Catholics and thus to thwart the widely held objective of many nationalists to get rid of partition by outbreeding the unionists. Discrimination had a political as well as an economic and social purpose and for many unionists was regarded as a legitimate response to what they perceived to be politically motivated opposition from the Catholic Church to most forms of birth control.

Since 1971 there has been a significant change in this demographic pattern towards a much more rapid growth in the overall proportion of Catholics. The precise figures are a matter for dispute given the reluctance of many heads of household to answer census questions on religion, as has already been seen. But it is clear that the proportion of Catholics in Northern Ireland has increased from a figure of at least 33 per cent in 1971 (31.4 per cent stated + some unstated) to a figure of at least 40 per cent in 1991 (38.4 per cent stated + some unstated). This increase is probably due, in part, to a continuing higher birthrate among Catholic families compared with Protestant families and, in part, to a relative decline in emigration among Catholics. That decline may in turn be due, in part, to an increase in job opportunities for Catholics within Northern Ireland and, in part, to a greater propensity among Protestants to emigrate. There is now clear evidence that substantially more Protestants than Catholics take up places in universities in Great Britain and that many of them do not return to seek permanent employment in Northern Ireland.[7] The corresponding figures for 1971 also included in Map 2.3 indicate that this increase in the proportion of Catholics has occurred throughout Northern Ireland with the exception of three districts in the Greater Belfast area where there was a slight decline – Carrickfergus, North Down and Ards – and two where there was no change – Coleraine and Down. It is also clear that the increase in the percentage of Catholics has been generally largest in western districts.

This relatively sudden change in the established population trends indicates how difficult it may be to predict future trends. It is possible to make some fairly accurate predictions on the likely growth or decline of one or other community on the basis of the balance between younger and older people, and particularly those of marriageable and child-bearing age. On this basis alone, it was and continues to be likely that the Catholic community, which has a much younger age profile and a tendency to have larger families, will continue to increase more quickly than the Protestant community, in which there is a larger proportion of older people and a tendency to have smaller families. For example, the 1991 census indicated that almost half (47 per cent) of the persons stated to be Catholics were under the age of twenty-five compared with only just over one-third (36 per cent) of the rest of the population.

The difficulty is that differences in fertility rates in different sections of the population can change,[8] and that differences in emigration rates can offset any actual increase in the number of births. During the 1970s demographers were divided on whether the observable decline in fertility in the Catholic community as Catholic households became more prosperous would continue to be sufficiently sustained to produce a measure of stability between the two communities in the absence of differential emigration rates. Some predicted that Catholics would become the majority community in a few decades, while others argued that there was likely to be a much slower increase and eventual stability.[9] In the period between 1971 and 1991 those who predicted a substantial increase in the proportion of Catholics proved to be right. It does not follow that this rate of increase is bound to continue. A major reason for the changing trend was that the demographic trend coincided with a major shift in emigration patterns which was attributable to socio-economic rather than demographic factors. The future balance in the numbers of the two major communities in Northern Ireland is dependent on many factors, not least the way in which the communal conflict develops or declines and the nature of any political settlement which may be reached. A substantial increase in paramilitary or communal violence would undoubtedly lead to an increase in emigration rates and also of internal population movements which might be greater than 'natural' demographic trends. All that can be stated with any certainty is that *if* present trends continue it can be expected that the numbers in the two major communities will become more equal within the next two decades. The political and other implications of this will then depend on whether policies directed towards greater separation or greater sharing have been pursued in the interim period, as will be argued in Part III of this book.

Residential segregation

A further major trend since 1971 has been a tendency for members of both major communities to congregate in areas where they feel safer and less exposed. This is most clearly observable in larger towns, where it has resulted in the development of large numbers of streets, housing estates or larger enclaves which are exclusively or almost exclusively populated by members of one or other community. It can be most easily illustrated in Belfast, where the areas or enclaves are larger and therefore appear clearly in the analysis of census returns in individual wards. The figures in Map 2.4 show that, in the majority of wards in the area, the population was highly segregated in the sense that fewer than 10 per cent declared themselves as members of the 'other' community, whether Protestant or Catholic. As has already been explained, however, it is not possible to give a completely accurate picture of the extent of segregation, since between 5 per cent and 25 per cent of heads of household refused to declare the religion of their families or said they had none. In many wards in communally exclusive parts of the city it is not unreasonable to assume that the population has been almost completely 'purified' by a mixture of actual or feared intimidation and the desire of most households to live in an area where they feel safe. But in some wards where a small minority is actually recorded the true extent of intermingling is likely to be somewhat higher, since members of the local minority may prefer not to reveal their religion. In others a high number in the 'none/not stated' categories may indicate a high proportion of people who reject any exclusive communal label.

It is not possible on the basis of published census figures to produce a corresponding chart for smaller urban and rural areas. But it is quite clear that in many towns and villages similar forces have been at work. Most public sector housing estates in larger towns have become exclusively or almost exclusively Protestant or Catholic, and the Northern Ireland Housing Executive has reluctantly accepted that most alloca- tions are in practice made on that basis. In Dungannon, for example, what used to be the only mixed estate in the town has recently become almost exclusively Catholic. Many streets in older parts of towns and villages have also become commu- nally exclusive. The 'colour' of estates, streets and sometimes of whole villages is immediately observable, both to casual observers and also to all who live there, from the decoration of kerbstones in red, white and blue, or green, white and orange, or by other sectarian wall paintings or signs. Even tourists in the scenic Mourne Mountains would have little difficulty in identifying the dominant community in the adjacent small towns of Hilltown and Rathfriland from the large signs at each entry proclaiming them to be respectively under the control of republicans and of loyalists. In most rural areas, however, the traditional attachment of families to their farms and the reluctance in both communities to sell land to the other side – reinforced by pressure from bodies like the Orange Order – appear to have been strong enough to preserve the established patterns. The main exception appears to have been in some border areas where there has been a withdrawal by some Protestant families to safer areas in the face of an allegedly deliberate policy on the part of the IRA to attack the owners or potential inheritors of isolated Protestant farms.

The obvious implication of these trends is that members of both communities prefer to live separately and to minimize their everyday contacts with members of the other community. But it is important not to generalize and to attempt to understand the pressures which lie behind the increasing separation. Many members of both communities and those in between continue to live happily and peacefully together in mixed areas. Map 2.4 also shows that in Greater Belfast there are many areas in which there is substantial and as yet relatively stable residential integration. Most, but not all, of these are in better-off suburbs and other areas which have not been affected by intercommunal confrontations or paramilitary activity. The pattern in other towns and villages and in rural areas is similar. Recent research indicates that at least one-third and perhaps up to one-half of Northern Ireland Housing Executive estates remain mixed.[10] And there is evidence that many people would prefer greater rather than less integration. An independent opinion survey carried out for the Northern Ireland Housing Executive in 1990 showed that two-thirds (65 per cent) of those questioned agreed that it should be the policy of the Housing Executive to ensure mixed religion in its estates; the responses on this question from existing tenants was slightly higher (71 per cent) than for non-tenants.[11]

Yet it is clear that the pressures which generate greater separation are generally stronger than the desire for integration. It takes only one brick through a window or one scribbled graffiti to make a family move out of a mixed into a safer area,

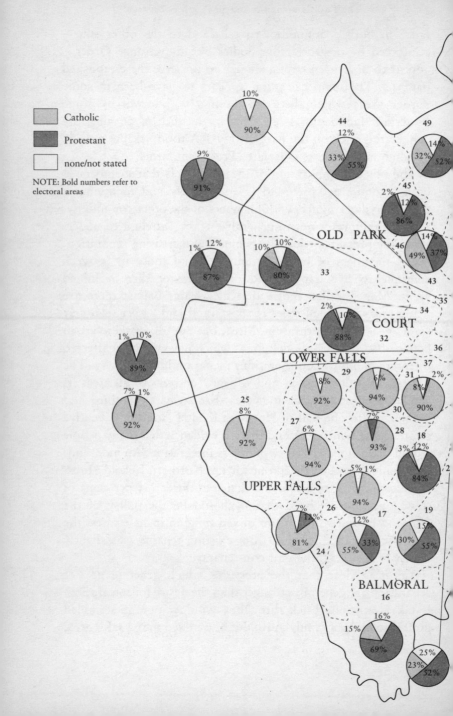

Catholic

Protestant

none/not stated

NOTE: Bold numbers refer to electoral areas

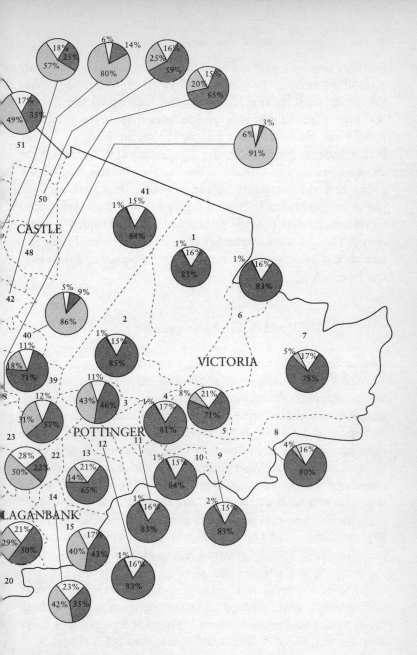

Map 2.4 *The distribution of Catholics, Protestants and people in between in Belfast in 1991*

however much they would have liked to stay. And it takes only a small minority of people in the area to carry out or provide the information for others to carry out such attacks or threats. It is often claimed that it is 'people from outside the area' who initiate the process. Thus far, as shown in research by the Policy Studies Institute in the late 1980s and confirmed by submissions to the Opsahl Commission, the reaction of the police and the Northern Ireland Housing Executive to these pressures has generally been to facilitate movement rather than to encourage and provide the backing for continued integration.[12] The question is whether the effects of intimidation and fear should be accepted as inevitable, or whether and how they can be resisted.

Social and cultural segregation

Residential segregation contributes to but does not of itself account for the continuing social and cultural separation between the two communities. There has always been a high degree of communal self-sufficiency and exclusiveness in social and sporting activities in Northern Ireland.[13] For many people these activities have traditionally been organized by or around their local churches. Most churches run social or indoor sports clubs and youth clubs on weekday evenings. Certain youth organizations such as the Boys and Girls Brigades are almost exclusively associated with Protestant churches. Organizations like the Scouts and Guides which are formally non-sectarian are also often loosely attached to particular churches, both Protestant and Catholic, and meet in their respective church halls. Since the level of regular attendance at church services and at other church-based activities remains high for both Protestants and Catholics, many families and individuals never have any real social contact with members of other churches.

Many other non-church activities are also effectively segre-

gated. The most exclusive on the Protestant side are the
Orange Order and the Royal Black Institution which together
have a membership of at least one hundred thousand and
which formally exclude any participation of any kind by
Roman Catholics. Since in many rural areas Orange Halls are
used as general purpose community centres, many local activities are effectively barred to Catholics. Masonic Lodges play a
similar role for the Protestant business community in some
towns. On the Catholic side the equivalent of the Orange
Order, the Ancient Order of Hibernians, is less strong. But the
Gaelic Athletic Association, which organizes all forms of Gaelic
sport, has a very large and active membership in most rural
areas with a substantial Catholic population. Though it does
not formally exclude Protestants, it makes its sympathies clear
by prohibiting participation by any member of the security
forces, though the ban on participation in non-Gaelic sports
such as rugby or football has been removed. Many of these
organizations provide drinking facilities on their premises and
are the centre of local social and communal activity. It is
highly unlikely that anyone who frequents any of these clubs or
premises will ever meet anyone from the other community there.

There are, of course, other social and leisure activities which
are not segregated. But many of them, such as concerts, theatres
and cinemas or swimming pools, do not involve any close or
sustained personal contacts with other users. Those that do,
such as business clubs like Rotary and the Lions, local history
clubs and cross-communal play or pressure groups, have a
relatively small membership and are often largely middle class.
Sustained contacts of this kind in working-class and rural areas
are often encouraged and assisted financially by such official
bodies as the Community Relations Council. But their membership and impact is also relatively small. So, too, is that of the
only substantial political party, the Alliance Party, which draws
its membership and activists from both communities. As a
result, even in areas where there is no very clear residential

segregation, there will often be no need or desire for contacts with neighbours from the other community to be other than polite but strictly at arm's length. And when social contacts are made it is usual for sensitive political and social issues to be avoided for fear of giving offence or sparking an argument.

Segregated and integrated education

The long-established segregation of the educational system in Northern Ireland also plays a significant part in maintaining the two communities as separate and mutually exclusive entities and in marginalizing contacts between them. The fact that almost everyone has attended a communally exclusive school means that very few have any school friends or contacts in the other community. It also permits children in both communities to grow up with a sense that people in the other community are essentially different. And it means that there is no need for teachers or children to face up to or question, in any serious way, the mutually exclusive views that are prevalent in both communities about their origins and history, the nature of the continuing conflict and of possible political accommodations between them.

The effective segregation of almost all primary and secondary schools throughout Northern Ireland stems from arrangements made in the 1920s.[14] Following partition in 1921 the new unionist government sought to develop a system of integrated schools for children from both communities. But in the face of sustained opposition from both the Catholic and the Protestant churches the plan was withdrawn and a deal was struck which was broadly acceptable to both sides. The Protestant churches agreed to transfer their primary schools to state control in exchange for full funding of both running and capital expenditure and a significant voice on their boards of governors. The Catholic Church was also granted full funding of the running expenditure of its primary schools, and was allowed to maintain formal ownership and control provided it agreed to raise a proportion of capital expenditure and to accept a minority of state nominees on its boards of governors. Similar arrangements were made for most grammar schools. The effect of this was that almost all Catholic children were catered for in exclusively Catholic schools – known as 'maintained schools' – under the direct control of the Catholic Church, while all Protestant children and a few Catholics who did not wish their children to be subjected to or labelled by a clerically dominated school system were catered for in 'state' or 'controlled' schools which were theoretically non-sectarian but were for practical purposes Protestant in character and outlook, or in maintained grammar schools of a similar character. The same structure was adopted in 1945 when secondary education became compulsory and new controlled and maintained secondary schools had to be provided for those who could not gain entry to grammar schools. It is still in place. And, since the policy of establishing comprehensive schools as in Britain has not been followed, so too is the 'eleven plus' selection test. The education system in Northern Ireland is thus dually segregated in that children are divided both by religion and by ability.

The provision of substantial government funding for Catholic schools for the minority Catholic population was in one sense one of the more liberal policies pursued under the Stormont regime. The right to establish and maintain its own schools is typically one of the primary demands of any religious, linguistic or cultural minority. The structures adopted for this purpose in Northern Ireland, however, have had the effect of imposing segregation on a substantial part of the population who wished to escape from this aspect of communal separation. Since the 1960s numerous opinion polls have consistently indicated that some two-thirds of respondents favoured integrated education and that up to half of parents would prefer their children to be educated in integrated schools. The initial response of the government was to ignore all such demands on the grounds that the opinion polls could not be taken seriously. It was not until groups of frustrated parents throughout Northern Ireland insisted on establishing their own integrated schools that the authorities began to take notice. The first new integrated school, Lagan College in Belfast, opened in 1981 and was soon followed by other voluntary foundations in other major towns. But all these schools had to establish their 'viability' over a number of years before the government would provide any funding. Eventually, in 1989, formal statutory provision was introduced to make state funding available for the establishment of new integrated schools and to facilitate the conversion of existing schools to integrated status. There are now eighteen integrated schools throughout Northern Ireland with roughly equal numbers of Protestants and Catholics and a total enrolment in 1993 of some 2,070 primary and 1,850 secondary children. But as the figures in Table 2.1 indicate, this is still a very small proportion of the total school population. And there is strong opposition to the creation of new integrated schools from the Roman Catholic bishops and some Protestant churches as well as from most established schools. The question which remains unanswered is whether many more parents would opt for integrated education if good quality integrated primary and secondary schools were available in every part of Northern Ireland, or whether most would prefer to remain in the existing segregated system. In this respect the evidence of successive opinion polls is that more people want integration than separation. The most recent survey, carried out in three areas in which there was already an integrated school, indicated that about 80 per cent of parents thought that it was important for Protestant and Catholic children to be educated together, though only between about a quarter and a half said they would be likely to send their children to the local integrated school.[15]

Table 2.1 *Segregated and integrated schools in Northern Ireland*

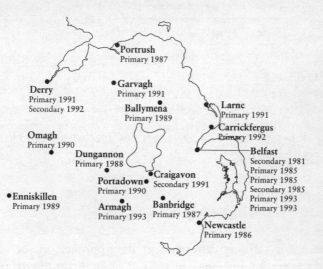

Portrush
Primary 1987

Derry
Primary 1991
Secondary 1992

Garvagh
Primary 1991

Ballymena
Primary 1989

Larne
Primary 1991

Carrickfergus
Primary 1992

Omagh
Primary 1990

Dungannon
Primary 1988

Belfast
Secondary 1981
Primary 1985
Primary 1985
Secondary 1985
Primary 1993
Primary 1993

Portadown
Primary 1990

Craigavon
Secondary 1991

Enniskillen
Primary 1989

Armagh
Primary 1993

Banbridge
Primary 1987

Newcastle
Primary 1986

Total enrolment (1992)	Protestant*	Catholic*	Integrated**
Primary	90,684	96,047	1,792 (2,070)
Preparatory	3,730		
Secondary (non-selective)	40,945	45,282	1,390 (1,850)
Grammar	33,192	23,678	

*These figures are for school management types; rather more Catholics attend Protestant schools than vice versa.

**The figures in brackets for integrated schools are for 1993.

Source: School Performance Information 1991/92, DENI (1993).

Table 2.2 *Unemployment rates*

	Protestants (%)		Catholics (%)	
	Male	Female	Male	Female
1971	7	4	17	7
1981	12	10	30	17
1985–7	14	9	36	15
1991	12	7	28	14

Source: Census reports for 1971, 1981 and 1991; continuous Household Survey data for 1985–7.

Discrimination in employment

There is a striking difference in the approach to segregation and integration in employment. The main thrust of governmental policy in this sphere is now to require all larger employers to use their best efforts to achieve a balanced workforce. This stems from the continuing concern over allegations of discrimination in employment between Protestants and Catholics. Since the creation of Northern Ireland – and probably for many years before – the unemployment rates for Catholics have been much greater than those for Protestants. The official figures for male unemployment in the Catholic community are currently more than twice those for Protestants and, as shown in Table 2.2, this differential has remained remarkably stable at least since 1971. Though the differential for women is much less, this is usually regarded as due as much to differences in the way the figures for female unemployment are measured as to any major difference in their treatment.

There is no doubt that during the period of unionist government there was some deliberate discrimination by employers, particularly in the public sector, not least with a view to maintaining the population balance between the two communities.[16] But there is also little doubt that some of the difference in unemployment rates stemmed from traditional employment patterns. Jobs in the professions, textiles, construction, catering and agriculture were fairly evenly divided. But jobs in banking, commerce, engineering and the police were regarded as being mostly for Protestants, and Catholic schools did not usually provide suitable qualifications for them. As a result, Catholics tended not to apply for them. Those that did find jobs in largely Protestant workplaces felt isolated and exposed and were subject to abuse or intimidation.

Fair employment legislation

Breaking down barriers of this kind has proved more difficult than was initially anticipated when legislation against discrimination in employment was first introduced in 1976. The new Fair Employment Agency initially concentrated its work on individual complaints of discrimination by employers. But relatively few complaints were made and it was very difficult to establish that there had been any deliberate discrimination. During the 1980s the Agency shifted the focus of its work to more general investigations of patterns of employment in major sectors or firms, notably the civil service, other public sector employers, the universities, banking and some major engineering firms. In almost every case it was found that more Protestants were employed than would have been expected and that some of the practices of employers were failing to give full equality of opportunity to Catholics. The results of this external monitoring, particularly in the case of the civil service, persuaded the government that more could be done by all employers to provide equality of opportunity if they were required to monitor the composition of their own workforces. A formal obligation to this effect, supervised by a strengthened Fair

Employment Commission, was imposed on all employers with more than twenty-five employees under an amending Fair Employment Act in 1989. The practical result is that, though there are no formal quotas for the numbers of Protestants or Catholics in any workforce, there is considerable pressure on employers to take action to secure a reasonable balance between them. One of the major achievements of the Fair Employment Agency and Commission has been to make it no longer acceptable in business circles to regard open or covert discrimination as either acceptable or unavoidable.

Segregation in employment

The results of the initial self-monitoring exercises by all larger employers have revealed that there is a major problem of segregation as well as of inequality in employment. In the case of many of the largest employers the imbalance in employment was shown to be relatively small. But there were many more workplaces than anticipated in which the workforce was exclusively or almost exclusively Protestant or Catholic and which in effect cancelled each other out in the overall communal employment figures. This pattern is particularly prevalent in smaller firms and workplaces and is likely to pose major difficulties when the obligation to monitor is extended to employers with fewer than twenty-five employees. For example, the monitoring returns for 1992 showed that 602 of the 843 smallest firms with between twenty-six and fifty employees and 209 of the 514 firms with between fifty-one and one hundred employees had fewer than ten Protestants or Catholics in their workforce, though the overall employment in all private sector firms with more than twenty-five employees was 62 per cent Protestant and 35 per cent Catholic, with 3 per cent undetermined.[17] The underlying question is whether there is an obligation on *all* employers to seek an appropriately balanced workforce or merely an obligation on the government to ensure that there is overall equality of opportunity and overall balance in employment and unemployment rates even if that is achieved by balancing substantial numbers of workplaces, which are wholly or predominantly Catholic or Protestant, against each other. Is equity in employment to be achieved within a framework of integration, as is currently assumed, or could it also be achieved in the context of increasing communal separation?

A particularly serious issue in this context is employment in the security forces and related services. This is one of the largest employment sectors in Northern Ireland, amounting in total to some 21,000 jobs. As will be seen in Chapter 3, some 11,500 are employed in the RUC and some 7,500 in locally recruited and locally deployed units of the Royal Irish Regiment, formally the UDR. The remainder are employed in the prison service and publicly financed security positions. In 1992, 87 per cent of these employees were drawn from the Protestant community, 7 per cent from the Catholic community and the remainder, many of whom are recruited in Great Britain, were classified as non-determined.[18] This is not due primarily to any lack of willingness on the part of the police, the Army or the prison service to recruit them, but to the general unwillingness among Catholics to work in the security forces or prison service. That, in turn, is due in part to a reluctance to work for the institutions of a state in which they feel alienated and ill-treated and in part to the fear of the reaction within their own community. The IRA and other republican paramilitaries make a point of targeting Catholic members of the RUC and the Army. It is generally accepted that it would be dangerous for a serving member of either to continue to live in predominantly nationalist areas such as West Belfast or even to visit them regularly when off duty. A decision by a Catholic to join the security forces may thus involve moving away from his or her community or family network into a safer area.

The significance of the continuing imbalance in employment

in this sector can be illustrated by showing how much it contributes to the overall imbalance in employment and unemployment in the two communities. For this purpose it is better to think in terms of actual numbers of persons employed or unemployed rather than differential percentages. For example, if the overall male unemployment rate is roughly 20 per cent and the rates for Protestants and Catholics are 13 per cent and 28 per cent, as was indicated in the 1991 census, this means that the differential is 2.1, i.e. that Catholic men are slightly more than twice as likely as Protestant men to be unemployed. If that is converted into actual numbers it means that roughly 26,000 Protestant males and roughly 36,500 Catholic males were unemployed. If employment in the 21,000 jobs in the security forces and related services was more equitably distributed, this would mean that about 7,500 more Catholics – and 7,500 fewer Protestants – would be employed. The effect of this on the overall figures would be that some 29,000 or 22 per cent of Catholic males would be unemployed compared with some 33,500 or 17 per cent of Protestant males, largely eliminating the differential. To achieve a similar reduction in the differential by creating jobs for Catholics without any corresponding reduction in Protestant employment would require the creation of some 14,000 new jobs.

This way of approaching the unemployment problem – in terms of numbers rather than differentials – also shows how dependent figures for differentials are on overall levels of unemployment. For example, if the overall unemployment rate for men could be reduced to 15 per cent, this would mean that, even if the differential remained at 2.1, some 11,000 fewer Catholics (26,000) and 8,000 fewer Protestants (18,000) would be unemployed. The effect of this would thus be almost identical, in terms of reducing the actual number unemployed in the Catholic community, to eliminating the differential, with overall unemployment remaining at 20 per cent. There may, therefore, be a significant difference in the policies which would be required to reduce the *differential* in unemployment rates as opposed to the policies required to reduce the *numbers* of unemployed in the Catholic community.

This brief account of some of the issues involved in assessing and dealing with differentials in employment and unemployment in the two communities shows how difficult it is to draw any simple conclusions. It is clearly inadequate in the light of the impact of employment in the security forces to conclude that deliberate or even unintended discrimination by employers is the only problem. The pressures for communal separation and the actions of paramilitaries on both sides also have a major impact on the willingness of Catholics to seek certain forms of employment. Even if those pressures can be reduced and full equality of opportunity and equity in employment between the two communities can be achieved in other sectors, the problem of the major differences in security employment may remain. It may also be difficult to achieve full equality in an economy in which the principle of separation in workplaces was accepted since that would make it even more difficult than at present to absorb the larger numbers of Catholics coming into the labour market as a result of larger family sizes in the Catholic community. Dealing with the unemployment problem cannot be treated in isolation from the political and security issues involved in the choice between policies based on the principles of separation or sharing.

Economic inequality

There is a direct and obvious link between employment patterns and general levels of household prosperity. If there is greater unemployment in the Catholic community, it is to be expected that Catholic households would have lower incomes than Protestant households. But equally significant differences in relative wealth and poverty are to be found within rather than between the two communities. There is, as always, a danger in jumping to conclusions based on an oversimplified two communities analysis.

The figures in Table 2.3 are intended to illustrate some of these complexities and to highlight the extent to which patterns of economic inequality in Northern Ireland differ from those in some other less prosperous regions of the United Kingdom and in the Republic of Ireland. The basic figures for gross household income show that while in 1987–8 the average household income in Northern Ireland at £225 per week was far below the United Kingdom average of £270, it was roughly the same as that for the North of England (£220), Wales (£228) and Scotland (£234) and for the Republic of Ireland (IR£248 = £220). The equivalent figures for 1992 show the Northern Ireland average of £281 somewhat further behind those in the same UK regions (North £285; Wales £295 and Scotland £314). But the pattern was not appreciably different.

The overall figures for Northern Ireland, however, conceal a substantial difference between those households which were recorded as Protestant, as Catholic and as neither. The figures for 1988 indicated an average income for Protestant households of £228 compared with an average of £185 for Catholic households and £247 for those not allocated to either. The figures for 1990 showed no such disparity between Protestant households (£253) and Catholic households (£253), though the unallocated households remained substantially better off (£324). The figures for 1992, however, show a continuing though somewhat smaller differential, with an average income for Protestant households of some £290 compared with a figure of £264 for Catholic households and £308 for unallocated households. The resulting income per head is further affected by the fact that the average Protestant household of 2.7 persons in 1988 and 2.5 in 1992 was slightly smaller than the average Catholic household of 3.3 persons in 1988 and 3.2 in 1992. These latter figures were slightly higher than the figures for UK regions and lower than that for the Republic of Ireland at 3.5 persons in 1987. On this basis it is easy to conclude that the incomes of Protestant families in Northern Ireland approximate to those of others in less well-off regions in the United Kingdom, while those of Catholic families are closer to those of families in the Republic of Ireland.

To focus attention exclusively on average income figures for Protestant and Catholic households in Northern Ireland in comparison with other regions may conceal as much as it reveals. A more significant and perhaps more realistic way of looking at figures for income may be to compare the range of incomes within each group so that a better picture can be given of the relative balance between the well-off, the comfortably off and the genuinely poor in each. The available figures on this indicate that household incomes are as unevenly distributed in Northern Ireland as in most other parts of the United Kingdom: in 1987–8 the Northern Ireland figures of 13 per cent for the highest income group (over £400 per week) and 32 per cent for the lowest income group (less than £100 per week) were not appreciably different from those for the North of England (14 per cent and 32 per cent), Scotland (15 per cent and 30 per cent) and Wales (13 per cent and 26 per cent); in 1990–91, though the categories had changed, the pattern was similar with 17 per cent in the highest income group (over £475) and 32 per cent in the lowest (less than £125) in Northern Ireland, compared with 14 per cent and 31 per cent in the North of England, 16 per cent and 29 per cent in Wales and 19 per cent and 32 per cent in Scotland. Equivalent though not exactly comparable figures for Protestant and Catholic households in Northern Ireland show a similar widely spread distribution, though there were, by a few percentage points, more Protestant households in the most prosperous group and a few less in the least prosperous group: in 1986–7 30 per cent of Protestant households were in the lowest group (less than £4,000 per year) and 16 per cent in the highest (more than

Table 2.3 *Relative prosperity in Northern Ireland, the Republic of Ireland and selected British regions*

2.3a *Gross household income and average household size in 1988 and 1992*

	1988			1992		
	Gross household income (£)	Average household size	Average per person (£)	Gross household income (£)	Average household size	Avera per perso
Northern Ireland						
Protestant	228	2.7	84	290	2.5	116
Catholic	185	3.3	56	264	3.2	83
Other	247	2.7	91	308	2.1	147
All	214	2.9	74	281	2.7	104
Great Britain						
North	220	2.5	88	285	2.5	114
Northwest	246	2.5	98	317	2.5	127
Wales	227	2.7	84	295	2.5	118
Scotland	234	2.5	94	314	2.4	131
Republic of Ireland	IR£248	3.5	IR£71			

2.3b *Percentages of households falling into highest and lowest income groups*

	1987–8 (%)		1990–91 (%)	
	less than £100 p.w.	more than £400 p.w.	less than £125 p.w.	more than £475 p.w.
Northern Ireland				
All	32	13	32	17
Great Britain				
North	32	14	31	14
Northwest	28	18	24	20
Wales	26	13	29	16
Scotland	30	15	32	19

Northern Ireland	1986–7 (%)		1988–90/91 (%)	
	less than £4,000 p.a.	more than £15,000 p.a.	less than £4,000 p.a.	more than £15,000 p.a.
Protestant	30	16	27	23
Catholic	39	9	30	17

Republic of Ireland	1987 (%)	
	less than IR£118 p.w.	more than IR£505 p.w.
All	30	20

Sources: *FES Monitor 2/93; Family Spending 1988, 1991, 1992 (UK); PPRU Monitor 2/92 & 1, 2/93 (NI); Household Budget Survey (RoI).*

£15,000 per year) compared with 39 per cent and 9 per cent of Catholic households; in 1988–91 the equivalent figures for Protestant households were 27 per cent and 23 per cent compared with 30 per cent and 17 per cent for Catholic households. It is clear from this that prosperity is as unevenly divided in both communities as elsewhere in the United Kingdom and that the differences within each community are far greater than those between them.[19]

Much of this is as might be expected. The social and economic structures in Northern Ireland are similar to those in other declining industrial areas in Britain. What is perhaps a little more surprising, at least to those who have not observed the very rapid growth of a prosperous Catholic middle class in Northern Ireland, is that the profiles of the two communities are so similar. One important consequence of this which is often overlooked is that, in purely numerical terms, there are more Protestant than Catholic households in the lowest income groups. The potential for alienation and disaffection associated with economic disadvantage is not therefore restricted to the Catholic community.

Voting patterns

A recent summary of the statistical evidence on voting patterns in Northern Ireland concluded that in terms of political solidarity the two communities were more clearly defined and stable in their allegiances than in other comparably divided societies in Europe.[20] The figures on voting in selected local, regional, Westminster and European elections set out in Table 2.4 bear this out: about 85 per cent of those who vote regularly give their first preferences to parties which are clearly identified as Catholic/nationalist or Protestant/unionist and only about 15 per cent to parties which promote themselves as cross-communal. This pattern holds good both in traditional 'first past the

	1973 (Assem)	1982 (Assem)	1987 (W'm)	1989 (Loc)	1989 (Eur)	1992 (W'm)	1993 (Loc)
Democratic Unionist (DUP)	11	23	12	18	30	13	17
Official Unionist (OUP)	29	30	38	31	22	34	29
Other unionists	22	6	5	5		3	3
(Total unionist)	62	59	55	54	52	50	49
Conservative		1	0	1	5	6	1
Alliance	9	9	10	7	5	9	8
Workers Party/Other labour	3	3	3	2	2		
(Total centre)	12	12	13	10	12	15	9
Social Democratic & Labour Party	22	19	21	21	25	24	22
Sinn Féin/Republican	3	10	11	11	10	10	12
(Total nationalist)	25	29	32	32	35	34	34
Other	1	1	0	4	1	1	6
Total	100	100	100	100	100	100	100
Percentage poll	72	60	67	56	48	70	55

Assem = Northern Ireland Assembly; W'm = Westminster Parliament; Loc = District Council; Eur = European Parliament

Source: Dr Sydney Elliott, Queen's University of Belfast

post' and in proportional representation elections. For example, in the most recent Westminster election in 1992 the main unionist parties secured 50 per cent of the vote, the main nationalist parties 34 per cent and centre parties 15 per cent; in the most recent district council elections in 1993 the equivalent figures were 49 per cent for the main unionist parties, 34 per cent for the nationalist parties and 9 per cent for the centre parties. The apparent solidity of these main voting blocks, however, masks some significant trends.

The first trend is the gradual increase in the strength of the nationalist block. During the 1970s the unionist block regularly accounted for about 60 per cent of the total vote compared with from 25 per cent to 30 per cent in the nationalist block and about 12 per cent in the centre block. Though the centre block appears to have remained relatively stable, there has been a significant shift by the 1990s of some 5 per cent to 10 per cent from the unionist to the nationalist block. The major reason for this is clearly the increase in the proportion of Catholics in the general population described above. But the re-emergence of Sinn Féin as the organized voice of republicanism has also played a part. In the 1970s there was no coherent party to represent those who supported traditional republican objectives. Though there were republican candidates of various descriptions in some constituencies, there was often little effective party organization and many traditional supporters must often have failed to vote, either from apathy or in pursuit of principled abstention. When Sinn Féin, in the wake of the widespread popular support for the IRA hunger strikers in 1981, abandoned their abstentionist position and decided on the dual strategy of 'taking power in Ireland with an Armalite in one hand and a ballot paper in the other', these hitherto concealed voters reappeared and boosted the total nationalist vote. The true position throughout the period was probably that the strength of the 'constitutional nationalists' in the SDLP led by John Hume was about double that of the republicans who were prepared to support or condone the use of armed force and to reject any objective short of British withdrawal.

A second significant feature has been the shifting of support among committed unionists between the long-established Ulster Unionist Party, currently led by Jim Molyneaux, and the Rev. Ian Paisley's Democratic Unionist Party (DUP). The more or less complete dominance of the Unionist Party within the Protestant community from the 1920s to the 1960s was initially threatened both by the emergence of the DUP as an organized party based on Paisley's Free Presbyterian Church in the early 1970s and by related divisions within the Unionist Party itself over the Sunningdale Agreement and the concept of power-sharing with the SDLP in 1973 and 1974. By the 1980s, the Unionists had restored a measure of party unity, despite their continuing internal differences over the desirability of restoring a devolved government in Northern Ireland as opposed to seeking more complete integration within the United Kingdom, and regularly secured about two-thirds of the unionist vote. But in times of political stress the DUP has been able to increase its support from its base of around 15 per cent to some 20 per cent, and in European elections, in which Northern Ireland is a single constituency and Ian Paisley has been able to capitalize on his personal popularity and larger-than-life personality, to around 30 per cent.

The centre block of some 15 per cent of those who vote for parties which promote themselves as cross-communal has also been somewhat variable. The Alliance Party, which is associated with the Liberal Democrats in Britain, regularly secures from 8 per cent to 10 per cent of votes, usually drawn more or less equally from both Protestants and Catholics. In district council and Assembly elections, held on a proportional representation basis, it also attracts lower preferences from both the unionist and nationalist blocks and thus secures a rather higher proportion of seats. The remainder of the centre block has in the past gone to socialist parties such as the Northern Ireland Labour Party (now defunct) and the Workers Party/Democratic Left and more recently to the Conservative Party. Much of the Conservative vote, however, has probably been drawn from voters who would otherwise have voted unionist or not at all. All the parties in this centre block, it should be noted, accept the current status of Northern Ireland as part of the United Kingdom.

Whatever the composition of this centre block it is clear on these figures that it is not strong enough to form a solid base for structures which require the sharing of power by representatives of both communities. The major imponderable in this context is whether, and if so how far, those who vote for the main unionist and nationalist parties are also prepared to support a power-sharing settlement.

Another major imponderable in any analysis of this kind is the allegiance of those who rarely or never cast their votes. Though a substantial proportion of the electorate typically refrains from voting, particularly in district council and European elections, it cannot be assumed that they would do so in the event of a constitutional referendum on a potential power-sharing or separation settlement or on Irish unification. There was a substantial number of non-voters on the nationalist side throughout the 1970s which has now emerged as part of the Sinn Féin vote, as has already been seen. It seems likely that there is an equally substantial number of non-voters on the unionist side who do not feel it necessary to vote in constituencies where there is a large unionist majority or who do not wish to support any of the main unionist parties. In the only formal referendum on the status of Northern Ireland as part of the United Kingdom held in 1973, 97 per cent of those who voted, comprising 58 per cent of the total electorate, voted to remain in the United Kingdom and less than 3 per cent, or 1 per cent of the total electorate, voted for a united Ireland. Since there was a deliberate policy of abstention on the part of the SDLP and other nationalist parties, it is not possible to draw any firm conclusions on what might happen if there was another border poll. It certainly cannot be assumed that the pattern in such a poll would be the same as in other recent elections. Nor can it be assumed that the votes in a referendum on other possible constitutional structures would divide on the same lines as in party elections.

Attitudes and aspirations

Some indication of the way in which the people as a whole might respond to such choices if they were formally asked can be obtained from the responses to opinion polls over the years. The attitudes of people in Northern Ireland on a wide range of issues are regularly surveyed, as elsewhere, both in commercial polls commissioned by newspapers and broadcasters and in more detailed academic research. In Northern Ireland these polls differ from those elsewhere only in that they are usually designed to contrast the opinion of members of the two communities and therefore tend to exclude the views of those who do not admit a communal affiliation, notably in polls based on quota samples of Catholics and Protestants. This limitation is probably offset, however, by the accepted tendency of those questioned to express somewhat less extreme positions than those which they may actually hold. None the less the polls, as elsewhere, have provided reasonably accurate predictions of party voting intentions in the run-up to elections and can therefore be taken to give a reasonably accurate guide to attitudes on other issues.

Apart from voting intentions the main focus of most opinion polls and most academic surveys has been on broader political and constitutional matters. At the simplest level there is a clear difference in the way in which Protestants and Catholics think of themselves. When asked to describe their national identity in the 1990 British Social Attitude Survey most Protestants described themselves as 'British' (66 per cent); about a quarter

(27 per cent) described themselves as 'Ulster' or 'Northern Irish'; and only a very few (4 per cent) described themselves as 'Irish'. Most Catholics, on the other hand, described themselves as 'Irish' (60 per cent); a similar number as 'Northern Irish' or 'Ulster' (27 per cent); and only one-tenth (10 per cent) as 'British'.[21] There has been a similar differential response to polls and surveys of attitudes towards the unification of Ireland. On this issue those categorized as Protestants have typically responded with almost unanimous opposition while those categorized as Catholics have been more divided. For example, in the Northern Ireland Attitude Survey carried out in 1978 only 4 per cent of Protestants favoured any form of united Ireland, while Catholics were almost equally divided between favouring various forms of unification (47 per cent) and various forms of settlement within the United Kingdom (50 per cent); and in the PSI Survey of Perceptions and Views carried out in 1986 only 5 per cent of Protestants favoured unification within the next thirty years while 80 per cent opposed it and 14 per cent expressed no preference; the corresponding figures for Catholics were 42 per cent in favour, 16 per cent opposed and 41 per cent no preference.[22]

When questions are asked on the best form of government within Northern Ireland there are divisions of opinion within both main communities, and on some issues a substantial measure of cross-communal agreement. In the 1978 Attitude Survey more than one-third of both Protestants (35 per cent) and Catholics (39 per cent) favoured a devolved power-sharing government within the United Kingdom; but while a similar proportion of Protestants (39 per cent) favoured devolved government with majority rule, only 1 per cent of Catholics agreed. And in an opinion poll on the recommendations of the Opsahl Commission carried out in 1993, 46 per cent of Protestants agreed or agreed strongly and only 34 per cent disagreed with the suggestion that a new government for Northern Ireland should be based on the principle of an equal voice for each community in making or vetoing laws and an equal share in administrative authority; among Catholics 86 per cent were in favour and only 3 per cent disagreed; when combined this produced an overall majority of 63 per cent in favour and only 26 per cent against.[23]

A similar mixture of shared and polarized opinions has been found in surveys and opinion polls on attitudes to the security forces and the legal system. For example, a *Belfast Telegraph* opinion poll on attitudes to the police in 1985 reported that while a substantial proportion of both Protestants (59 per cent) and Catholics (43 per cent) said they thought the RUC carried out its duties fairly, the rest of the Protestants (37 per cent) said that the RUC carried out its duties very fairly, while the rest of the Catholics (53 per cent) said that it carried out its duties unfairly or very unfairly. A similar question in the PSI Survey of Perceptions and Views in 1986 on the performance of the British Army found that a clear majority of both Protestants (85 per cent) and Catholics (68 per cent) felt that the Army treated Protestants and Catholics equally, though a substantial minority of Catholics (28 per cent) felt that the Army treated Protestants better. Views on the fairness of the legal system as a whole were similarly divided: in the *Belfast Telegraph* opinion poll two-thirds of Protestants said they thought the system was fair (64 per cent) and one-third thought it unfair (34 per cent), while two-thirds of Catholics said they thought it was unfair (68 per cent) and one-third fair (32 per cent). Even higher levels of polarization can be found on a few issues, such as the use of plastic bullets: in the same poll most Catholics (87 per cent) said their use was unacceptable while most Protestants (86 per cent) said they were acceptable. But this level of disagreement is exceptional. On most issues of this kind about half of those who were questioned in each community, and sometimes more, shared the same attitudes.

An even higher level of shared attitudes can be found on many social and moral issues. Members of both communities in Northern Ireland differ from people in the rest of the United Kingdom in their attitudes to such issues as pre-marital sex, homosexuality, artificial insemination and measures against pornography. On all these issues people in Northern Ireland from both communities expressed significantly more conservative opinions in the British Social Attitude Survey of 1990 than even church-going respondents in Britain. For example, 30 per cent of people in Northern Ireland said that pre-marital sex was always wrong compared with 12 per cent in Great Britain; and some 70 per cent said that the law should prohibit abortion on purely economic or social grounds compared with some 40 per cent in Great Britain. On matters of this kind the only major difference between Protestants and Catholics in Northern Ireland was in respect of attitudes to abortion; for example, 62 per cent of Catholics were opposed to abortion if there is a strong chance of a defect in the baby compared with only 19 per cent of Protestants.[24]

These results indicate that, while on some matters opinion is sharply polarized and supports a simple two-communities analysis, there are many others on which opinion is as divided within as between the two communities and on which there is a considerable degree of convergence in the centre. On these issues the two communities overlap to such an extent that it becomes questionable whether it is not better to say that there is a large community of opinion in the centre and two much smaller communities with sharply polarized views on the extremes.

Only two communities?

In the light of this summary of the evidence on political, economic and social differences within Northern Ireland, it is hard to deny that two distinct communities can be defined and identified on a wide range of overlapping characteristics. Protestants and Catholics in Northern Ireland do not merely attend different churches. They have differing perceptions of their national identity, they vote for different political parties and express sharply polarized views on such matters as the use of plastic bullets. On the other hand, there are many matters on which the differences between Protestants and Catholics are very much less, notably in their economic characteristics and their views on such matters as integrated education and the desirability of sharing power in government. On matters of this kind the overlap in characteristics and attitudes is much greater than the differences. On some of these matters a clear majority of both Protestants and Catholics share identical characteristics and attitudes. There is also a minority of people in Northern Ireland who cannot properly be described as either Protestants or Catholics or who do not wish to be categorized as belonging to either the Protestant or the Catholic community.

One way of attempting to summarize the position is to describe the characteristics of the two main communities, taking account of the wide variety of social and economic conditions and the equally wide range of opinion within each.

On this basis the Protestant community can be said to constitute about 50 per cent of the total population in Northern Ireland. It is heavily concentrated in and around Belfast and the surrounding areas of County Antrim and the north of Counties Down and Armagh, and many of its members in urban areas live in estates and suburbs that are increasingly segregated. Though it spans the whole range of employment and unemployment and economic prosperity and hardship, its members have slightly higher-status employment and are slightly better off than their counterparts in the Catholic community. Though in rural areas there is less obvious segregation, Protestant farmers tend to have somewhat larger and more productive holdings that are concentrated on the better land in the eastern counties and in the river valleys in western counties. Most members of the Protestant community regard themselves as British or Northern Irish rather than Irish, and are almost unanimous in their rejection of any form of Irish unification or any moves towards it. On other constitutional and political issues they are divided between hardline and more liberal attitudes. Those who vote for Rev. Ian Paisley's Democratic Unionist Party and some who vote for the Official Unionist Party are opposed to any form of power-sharing with nationalists and favour military and legal measures against terrorists. But others who support the Official Unionists and the Alliance Party appear willing to accept political compromise on power-sharing and other matters.

The Catholic community can be said on a similar basis to constitute about 40 per cent of the total population in Northern Ireland. Since Catholic families tend to be a little larger than Protestant families that proportion is slowly growing. It is concentrated in West Belfast, in the western counties of Londonderry, Fermanagh and Tyrone and in the southern parts of Counties Armagh and Down. Though some of its members have always experienced higher levels of unemployment and poverty than comparable people in the Protestant community, others have secure employment, much of it in the public and professional sectors, and enjoy comparable standards of living with Protestants in those sectors. Most Catholics regard themselves as Irish and have an aspiration towards the unification of Ireland. But a substantial minority either favour or are content with the current status of Northern Ireland as part of the United Kingdom, not least on economic grounds. Just over half of Catholic voters support John Hume's Social Democratic and Labour Party which seeks to achieve the unification of Ireland by peaceful means; about one-third support Sinn Féin, which is the political counterpart of the Provisional IRA, though not all of those are in favour of all aspects of the IRA campaign; the remainder support cross-communal and broadly unionist parties like Alliance. The vast majority appear to support the concept of a power-sharing government for Northern Ireland under a constitution which recognizes the validity of nationalist aspirations.

An alternative way of summarizing the same set of facts is to say that the two main communities are much less all-embracing and that there is between them a substantial body of people who cannot or do not want to be categorized in that way. These include at least three main groups:

1 Those who have no direct association with either main community, notably those from Britain and abroad, or who have deliberately abandoned any communal associations;

2 Those who have close associations and sympathies with both communities, notably those involved in mixed marriages or with other close relations in both communities;

3 The larger number of people who can readily be allocated to one or other community for some purposes but who reject many of the prevailing attitudes in those communities and who want to be left to get on with living peacefully together.

The proportion of the population which can be said to form part of this third community is quite fluid, though in theory no more so than that of the two main communities. For some purposes, such as answering census questions on religion or voting for the Alliance and other cross-communal parties, it can be quite small, usually between 5 per cent and 15 per cent. For other purposes, which do not involve a total rejection of all aspects of association with the main Protestant and Catholic communities in their broadest sense, such as expressing a desire for integrated education, greater integration in housing or for power-sharing in government or a distaste for traditional sectarian politics, it can be much larger and may be the largest of the three communities.

It is not, of course, possible to come to any firm conclusion on which of the two descriptions – a simple two-communities analysis or the more fluid multi-communal approach – is the more accurate. In times of greatest stress or fear, for example when the level of paramilitary violence is high or when there is more than usual constitutional uncertainty, many people who would normally act or vote as members of the central group feel more ready to accept that they belong to the more

exclusive Protestant or Catholic communities. But many feel
that they are being forced into this form of communal separation by circumstances beyond their control and might accept
the opportunity to express their support for communal sharing
if it were open to them to do so. In this sense the correct
description of the nature of the communities in Northern
Ireland is dependent on the actions and policies of others, the
paramilitaries, the leaders of the main political parties and the
British and Irish governments. One way of resolving the issue
may be to allow the people themselves to choose by the use of
the referendum strategy suggested in Chapter 8.

CHAPTER 3

The Armed Struggle

Northern Ireland is presented in the media as a place where daily life is dominated by shootings and bombs. Almost the only coverage in national and international television and newspapers until the recent peace initiatives has been of major terrorist incidents. Local news bulletins and newspapers within Northern Ireland are also dominated by reports of the many other less spectacular incidents which do not attract the attention of outsiders. Most visitors are struck on their first arrival by the frequent sight of soldiers and police with guns at the ready walking the streets or manning road blocks. Yet for all but a significant minority in Northern Ireland life apparently goes on more or less completely unaffected by these reminders of the continuing conflict in their midst. Many visitors are also struck by the way in which people go about their business as if the heavily armed army and police patrols which pass close by were invisible.

One issue which this odd juxtaposition raises is whether the conflict is as serious as it is made out to be and whether it has much impact on the way ordinary people think and behave. That in turn raises the issue of the influence which the paramilitary bodies and the security forces directly involved in it have on possible future developments. Should the objective of security policy be merely to contain the conflict until a political settlement can be worked out? Or are the paramilitaries on either side so central to the problem that they must be included in any workable settlement? There is also the issue of whether the methods currently used by the security forces are likely to succeed even in containing the conflict rather than making it worse. And if they are making it worse, how best can they be altered and controlled?

It may seem unnecessary to focus attention on the armed conflict at a time when the prospects of peace are said to be the best for twenty-five years. An understanding of the way in which the IRA and loyalist paramilitaries think and operate, however, is as important to the search for peace as an understanding of other aspects of the conflict. And a lasting peace has not as yet been achieved. Even if there is a reduction or cessation of paramilitary activity during the continuing discussions over the Downing Street Declaration, the possibility that in the event of a breakdown the campaigns by paramilitaries will be resumed cannot be ignored.

The best way to describe the experience in both communities of two decades of paramilitary violence and of heavy state security may be to combine some hard facts and statistics with some more subjective descriptions of how the conflict has been typically pursued and what it has meant in practice on the ground: the pattern of terrorist attacks and the typical response by the security forces; the nature of the paramilitary bodies involved and their methods of operation; the methods used by the Army and the police in attempting to prevent attacks from occurring and to find out and deal with those responsible; and the national and international legal standards which govern all sides.

The paramilitary campaigns

The initial stages of the current conflict in Northern Ireland were dominated by direct confrontations between unruly crowds of Protestants and Catholics or between crowds and the police or the Army. Most of these confrontations or riots took place in nationalist areas in larger towns and many were directly associated with planned public demonstrations or marches. This kind of conflict is now much less common, though there are occasional disturbances during paramilitary funerals and on the fringes of controversial marches. The most serious recent example was several nights of rioting in a loyalist area of Belfast in July 1993 following the death of a paramilitary steward who blew himself up with his own grenade which he was supposedly carrying to protect Orangemen from attack by republicans. These disturbances, during which about twenty vehicles were burned, were reportedly orchestrated by loyalist paramilitaries. In this, as in other matters, the loyalist paramilitaries have been adopting long-established IRA tactics. For many years riots of this kind were mounted in nationalist areas to mark the anniversary of the introduction of internment on 9 August 1971.

The most common form of incident now is a shooting attack by paramilitaries, either on members of the security forces by IRA units or on individual Catholics by loyalist units. In 1993, as in most of the 1980s, there were about 500 shootings of this kind, or one or two every night, as shown in Table 3.1. But many of the 200 or 300 incidents recorded in most recent years as bomb attacks are also essentially similar, in that they involve throwing a small bomb – a grenade or what is known as a coffee-jar bomb – at an Army or police patrol or at a Catholic house. There are fewer really large bomb attacks, perhaps ten or twenty successful explosions a year and as many that are defused or otherwise aborted. But these overall figures conceal some important differences in the targets and methods of operation of the IRA and their loyalist counterparts, the Ulster Volunteer Force (UVF) and the Ulster Defence Association (UDA) under its various cover names, notably the Ulster Freedom Fighters (UFF).

On the republican side, the main focus of attack is on the security forces as the primary symbol of what the IRA regard as an illegitimate British presence in Ireland. But no distinction

Table 3.1 Incidents, injuries and deaths arising from the 'troubles', including attributed responsibility for deaths, 1969–93

Year/Period	Shootings	Bombs	Injuries	Deaths					Responsibility (%)		
				Army	UDR	RUC/R	Civil	All	Rep.	Loy.	Sec.
1969	73	10	765	–	–	1	12	13			
1970	213	170	811	–	–	2	23	25			
1969–70 (av) (riots)	143	81	838	–	–	1	17	19			
1971	1,756	1,515	2,592	43	5	11	115				
1972	10,628	1,853	4,876	103	26	17	321	467			
1973	5,018	1,520	2,651	58	8	13	171	250			
1974	3,206	1,383	2,398	28	7	15	166	216			
1975	1,803	691	2,474	14	6	11	216	247			
1976	1,908	1,428	2,729	14	15	23	245	297			
1971–76 (av) (internment)	4,053	870	2,935	43	11	15	206	275	50	32	12
1977	1,081	1,143	1,387	15	14	14	69	112			
1978	755	748	985	14	10	7	50	81			
1979	728	624	875	38	10	14	51	113			
1980	642	402	801	8	9	9	50	76			
1981	1,142	578	1,350	10	13	21	57	101			
1977–81 (av)	870	532	1,080	17	11	14	55	97	70	14	10

1984	334	258	866	9	10		36	64			
1985	237	251	916	2	4		25	54			
1982–85 (av) (supergrass strategy)	386	321	704	9	8	16	41	73	70	11	13
1986	392	275	1,450	4	8	12	37	61			
1987	674	393	1,130	3	8	16	66	93			
1988	537	466	1,047	21	12	6	54	93			
1989	566	427	959	12	2	9	39	62			
1990	559	320	906	7	8	12	49	76			
1986–90 (av) (Anglo-Irish Agreement)	546	376	1,098	9	8	11	49	77	66	22	8
1991	499	604	962	5	8	6	75	94			
1992	506	497	1,066	4	2	3	76	85			
1993	476	289	826	6	2	6	70	84			
1991–93 (av) (talks process)	494	463	955	5	4	5	74	88	45	48	6

Notes: Rep. = republican paramilitaries; Loy. = loyalist paramilitaries; Sec. = security forces; RUC/R = RUC or RUC Reserve; UDR = Ulster Defence Regiment, recruited exclusively within Northern Ireland (amalgamated in 1992 with the Royal Irish Regiment); Army = British Army regiments recruited in Great Britain.

There is some variation in the figures compiled by different bodies. In this tabulation figures for shootings, bombs and deaths are taken from RUC Annual Reports; those for casualties are from Northern Ireland Office press releases; attributions of responsibility for deaths are adapted from figures compiled on a slightly different basis by the Irish Information Partnership for the period from 1969 to 1989, updated from 1990 by RUC attributions; killings for which no firm attribution could be made are not displayed in the tabulation, but are included in the calculation of the percentages.

The periods for which averages have been calculated have been chosen to illustrate the main phases of the conflict as explained in the accompanying text.

is made for this purpose between British soldiers and locally recruited police and soldiers who are also regarded as defenders of an illegitimate partition of Ireland. Relatively few of the nightly shooting attacks on security force patrols, however, cause death or serious injury, since most appear to be carried out by relatively inexperienced volunteers and since individual soldiers and policemen and their vehicles are reasonably well protected. Most of the fatalities or serious injuries are caused by more carefully planned attacks. One common method is to put a small semtex bomb under the car of an off-duty member of the security forces. Another is to detonate a much larger bomb hidden in a culvert or behind a wall as a patrol passes by. This usually involves laying a wire or a short-wave radio link to the hidden bomb and positioning young scouts to alert a more experienced IRA member at a detonation point to the approach of the patrol. A third common form of attack is the use of mortar bombs directed at police and army bases. Though a few of these have hit their target and caused multiple deaths and injuries, many have missed or failed to explode. Police and Army bases have also been attacked by driving very large car, van or tractor bombs close to their perimeter walls. Some of these – known as proxy bombs – have been carried out by forcing civilians on threat of death to drive the car or van to its target. More recently some have been directed by various forms of remote control. The latest development during 1993 has been the use in border areas of long-distance sniper shots from a high-powered and highly accurate rifle. By means of these different and constantly changing forms of attack, the IRA has succeeded in killing about twenty or thirty soldiers and policemen a year since the early 1980s – a substantial reduction from the average of over fifty per year during the 1970s.

The IRA has also been responsible for many attacks on civilians, including politicians, though its spokesmen and supporters like to play down this side of its activities. Since the mid-1980s it has adopted a policy of assassinating civilian employees and managers of businesses alleged to be working for or supplying the security forces. It has also assassinated a number of persons suspected of being involved in loyalist paramilitary groups, though in a number of cases the 'wrong' person has been killed. A substantial proportion of the civilian victims of the IRA, however, have been individuals in nationalist communities who are suspected of being informers or of being involved in anti-social activity. Alleged informers are summarily executed at the rate of two or three per year. Every year about one hundred youths are beaten or 'kneecapped' – shot through one or both knees – as a punishment for burglaries, joyriding or drug trafficking in nationalist areas. Random attacks have also been made on civilians in Protestant areas, usually in retaliation for loyalist attacks on Catholics. Though attacks of this kind are sometimes condemned as illegitimate and sectarian by the IRA command, it is widely believed that some of them are carried out by IRA units on an 'unofficial' basis. Others have been carried out by other smaller republican paramilitary bodies, such as the Irish National Liberation Army (INLA). The IRA is also suspected of having organized attacks or threats against any remaining Protestant families in some predominantly nationalist areas with a view to forcing them to move out and make way for Catholic families. Its operations are financed by various forms of armed robbery, extortion, and racketeering.

The third main aspect of IRA activity is its sustained campaign against commercial property. The two most common forms of attack are large car or van bombs placed in urban centres and tiny incendiary devices placed inside shops and stores. In 1991 and 1992 there was a sustained campaign of incendiary attacks. More recently the focus has shifted back to huge town-centre bombs which have devastated the commercial centres of Lurgan, Coleraine, Bangor, Portadown, Newtownards, Magherafelt, Armagh and some streets in central

Belfast. These types of bomb have caused very substantial damage, both in Northern Ireland and in Britain, and the cost of reconstruction and compensation has increased very substantially. The average annual figure for official compensation payments in recent years within Northern Ireland has been some £40 million. The cost of compensation for recent bombs in the City of London has been estimated at more than £1 billion.

The pattern of attacks by loyalist paramilitaries is very different. Unlike the IRA they have no ideological or political reason for attacking British soldiers or the police or for bombing commercial targets. Their campaign is directed primarily against what they regard as the nationalist threat to the continued existence of Northern Ireland as part of the United Kingdom. In practice this results in a mixture of planned attacks on persons suspected of being involved in the IRA or other republican paramilitary bodies and of more or less random attacks on civilians in nationalist areas. Most of the directed attacks are made by shooting or throwing bombs into the houses of those suspected of being paramilitaries. Since 1992 this category of target has been expanded to include nationalist politicians, in particular Sinn Féin councillors and party members, on the ground that they are involved in a 'pan-nationalist conspiracy'. There have been persistent allegations of security force collusion in some of these attacks.[1] Random attacks in nationalist areas typically involve firing shots from a passing car or motorcycle at people standing on the street or mounting a bomb or machine gun attack on customers in a pub or betting shop. In recent years the number of casualties from loyalist terrorism has risen sharply, as indicated in Table 3.1. More than one-half of all killings related to the conflict in 1993 were attributed by the RUC to loyalists compared with less than one-quarter in the 1980s.[2]

Loyalist paramilitaries are responsible for large numbers of punishment shootings and beatings in their own areas. This activity, like the corresponding operations of the IRA, is directed in part at deterring members of their own organization from acting as informers or otherwise cooperating with the security forces and in part at asserting their authority within their own communities. Loyalist paramilitaries also organize threats and attacks on any remaining Catholic families or mixed marriages in their area. Like republican paramilitaries, they are directly or indirectly involved in both lawful and unlawful drinking clubs and in extracting large sums of 'protection money' from businesses and from contractors and workers on building sites where they can make credible threats.

Who is involved?

It is obviously difficult to be sure exactly who is directly or indirectly involved in terrorist operations. Though security force sources and commentators sometimes claim to know the names of all the leading activists, the reality is that no one knows precisely who is controlling the various paramilitary groups at any one time. But enough is known of their general organization and of the kind of person who becomes active at lower levels, notably from studies of those who are dealt with in court, to give a reasonably accurate picture of the extent of active involvement and passive support for paramilitary groups on either side.

The most active and well-organized group is the Provisional IRA. It claims to be the descendant of the original Irish Republican Army which fought the British Army in Southern Ireland in the period from 1916 to 1921. It mounted further but wholly ineffective campaigns in Northern Ireland and Britain in 1939 and 1956–62. Its leaders and most of its adherents are committed not only to finishing the job of driving the British out of Ireland but also to an analysis of the conflict which stresses the problem of the British presence in

Ireland and plays down the existence of a Protestant community in Northern Ireland that is vehemently opposed to Irish
unification. The use of the word Provisional – to distinguish it
from the Official IRA – stems from one of the many splits in
the republican movement. In 1970 the Provisionals broke away
from the then dominant left-wing group which was moving
away from the traditional nationalist analysis and had declared
that it was abandoning the use of force, though it continued to
maintain a military wing known as the Official IRA.

The 'Provisionals' or 'Provos' – though these abbreviations
are now giving way even among nationalist graffiti writers to
the British Army designation 'PIRA' – were initially organized
on quasi-military lines with battalions and a well-defined hierarchy of officers and volunteers in each county or town area.
But it was soon found that this structure made it too easy for
intelligence officers in the security forces to obtain the names
of IRA officers and volunteers from informers. In its place a
simpler cell structure has been developed in which the members
of each active service unit know only the identity of their
immediate colleagues, thus making it much more difficult for
the police to identify or obtain evidence against those in
control of the supply of weapons and of tactics. The leadership
appears to be drawn mainly from a number of traditional
republican families whose members have been involved in
paramilitary activity for many years. Estimates of the numbers
in active service units at any one time vary from a few hundred
to more than a thousand. But it is probably impossible to be
precise on such matters given the wide range of degrees of
involvement.

This is perhaps best explained by describing the typical
processes of recruitment, in which the desire for excitement
and prestige amongst friends and harassment by security force
patrols both play a part. Youngsters in nationalist areas may
begin by selling An Phoblacht, a republican weekly newspaper
which contains a good deal of IRA propaganda. They may

then graduate to membership of Fianna Éireann which may involve acting as scouts for simpler attacks on Army or police patrols or assisting in punishment operations – beatings with hurley sticks and perhaps kneecappings. At some stage they will be given some training in the use of weapons and explosives and in resisting interrogation by the police. Those who carry out these simple tasks effectively, and without any suspicion of loose talking or cooperation of any kind with the security forces, may then be asked to join an active service unit by assisting in the delivery or hiding of firearms and explosives or acting as a driver. Then, sometimes without advance warning, they may be asked to lay a bomb or act as trigger man in an assassination or execution. Those who have been fully 'blooded' in this way may then find it increasingly difficult to withdraw, even if they want to. The punishments for failing to carry out orders are severe and any suspicion of informing or 'touting' may lead to summary execution. The only way out of involvement may be to confess and serve a term of imprisonment or to seek the assistance of one of the peace groups which try to help those under threat to find a safe refuge and livelihood in Britain or the Republic.

Similar threats and punishments are used against people in nationalist areas who become involved in IRA activities against their will: those who are asked or required to allow their houses or sheds to be used for storing weapons, or to make their car available for an operation, or even to deliver a car bomb. Any suspicion of cooperation with the RUC or Army in such cases, whether by using the confidential telephone, by giving evidence against IRA members or failing to deliver the car bomb as instructed may lead to – or be thought to be likely to lead to – attacks on the individual concerned or his or her family and may force the family to move elsewhere. Many prefer to cooperate, however unwillingly, and to plead duress if they are found out.

The pattern of involvement in other republican groups, such

as the Irish National Liberation Army and the Catholic Reaction Force, is less clear. Many of those involved in the INLA had probably been involved in the Provisional IRA at some time before the INLA broke away in 1974. INLA activists have thus tended to be older and more experienced. Much of their activity has involved attacks directed against loyalist paramilitaries or internal republican feuding. In some cases it has involved retaliation against Protestant civilians which would not be officially authorized or acknowledged by the Provisionals. In 1991 and 1992, however, the Provisionals carried out a sustained campaign against rival groups, notably the Irish People's Liberation Organization (IPLO), and their activities have since declined to negligible proportions. Some retaliatory action against Protestant areas may also be carried out by Provisional IRA members using INLA or the Catholic Reaction Force as badges of convenience.

The organization and membership of loyalist paramilitary groups are generally regarded as less well developed and more fluid than those of the Provisionals. The Ulster Volunteer Force (UVF) emerged as a small and highly secretive terrorist group in the 1960s which took over the historically emotive name of the mass movement of Protestants against Home Rule in 1912. The Ulster Defence Association (UDA) was in a sense the true successor of the original UVF in that it rose out of the reaction of Protestants in working-class areas in 1972 against what was perceived as a threat of a British sell-out. Until 1991 the UDA remained a lawful organization. Its initial stated objective was the mobilization of large numbers of loyalists in opposition to any form of Irish unification, though some of its members were involved in large numbers of sectarian murders in the early 1970s. In the late 1970s and early 1980s it developed a more political strategy under the leadership of Andy Tyrie and produced a series of proposals for a form of independence for Northern Ireland in which Catholics were promised a share of power. But other UDA members continued to carry out a policy of responding to IRA killings and bombings with attacks on Catholic civilians under various flags of convenience, notably that of the Ulster Freedom Fighters (UFF). From 1990 this wing of the organization became dominant, and the UDA was finally declared unlawful in 1991 following a particularly savage machine-gun attack on a Catholic betting shop.

At about the same time the main loyalist groups began to coordinate their strategy and to respond to IRA activities and political developments with statements and threats from what they called their 'joint command'. This development confirmed what many already suspected, that membership of the UVF and the UDA or UFF was, if not interchangeable, at least somewhat intermixed. It appears that until recently most operations in the Belfast area were carried out without much advance planning by small groups based in loyalist drinking clubs and pubs and that many of those involved were younger and had less experience and expertise with firearms and explosives than their IRA counterparts. This may be linked with their choice of soft civilian targets, as opposed to the technically sophisticated defences of the Army and police patrols and bases chosen as targets by the Provisionals. In country areas on the other hand, notably in North Armagh and Tyrone, the active units appear to have been somewhat more permanent and tightly organized and to have planned and directed their attacks with rather more care. Some of those involved in these groups are clearly older and more experienced and have probably had the advantage of military discipline and weapons training as members of the Ulster Defence Regiment (UDR). It is also alleged that they have acted in collusion with serving members of the security forces. More recently, under the new coordinated UVF and UDA/UFF command, it has been reported that a cell structure similar to that of the Provisionals has been adopted. Recent operations in Belfast have been carried out with greater sophistication and planning against selected targets rather than randomly against the civilian population in nationalist parts of the city. This suggests a smaller and more carefully selected membership. It has also been reported that in 1993 a wider recruitment drive directed at younger people was launched in loyalist communities in the Belfast area.

Soldiers or criminals?

These sketches of paramilitary activity and recruitment on either side point towards another significant aspect of the conflict – that those involved are not, as is sometimes implied by government ministers or the press, habitual criminals or in some way psychologically disturbed. Most are broadly representative of the communities from which they come. They are more like young soldiers who have joined an army, partly because they believe in the cause they are fighting for, partly in search of prestige and excitement and partly because it provides employment in areas where jobs are hard to come by. In some of these respects they are not unlike those who join the British Army and who are deployed against them.

This view is borne out by two parallel studies of the backgrounds and previous records of those who have appeared before the courts on terrorist charges in 1975 and 1989–90.[3] In both surveys the majority of defendants at the time of their offences were young males. Most had either no previous criminal record (in 1989–90 33 per cent of nationalist offenders and 20 per cent of loyalists) or what was classified as a non-serious record of minor property or public-order offences (in 1989–90 41 per cent of nationalists and 36 per cent of loyalists). A substantial proportion of both (in 1989–90 46 per cent of loyalists and 33 per cent of nationalists) were employed at the time of their arrest. The author of the 1989–90 survey concluded that 'most of those who are now actively engaged in the political violence in Northern Ireland seem to be men, between the ages of seventeen and twenty-five, who have "working-class" backgrounds and differ little from a large number of other people in the region in terms of their educational achievement, employment or criminal records'.

The extent of communal support

If those involved in paramilitary operations on both sides are reasonably representative of their respective communities in urban and rural areas, as this evidence suggests, can they also rely on support or at least acquiescence from their communities? The evidence on this is somewhat equivocal and probably gives a fairly accurate picture of ambivalent and changeable attitudes on the ground.

The degree of communal support for 'their' paramilitaries is clearly greatest in committed nationalist and loyalist areas. In Belfast, these include on the republican side the Lower Falls, Ardoyne and New Lodge, and on the loyalist side the Shankill Road and some outer housing estates; and in the country they include south Armagh, south Fermanagh and east Tyrone on the republican side, and parts of north Armagh and east Tyrone on the loyalist side. Voting patterns, turnout for demonstrations and even participation in riots over the years indicate that support is not a result of intimidation but of the perception that the IRA or the UDA or UVF are the only people who will defend the community – or carry out effective retaliation – against attacks from the other side. But a series of studies by sociologists who have lived in areas of this kind have stressed that the degree of support and acquiescence is quite variable: that a substantial minority of the community in nationalist areas, especially those with deep religious commitment, is opposed to paramilitary activity of any kind and that the degree of support from others is conditional on what the paramilitaries do.[4] In the Lower Falls in the early 1980s, for example, a sample survey of households revealed that about half those interviewed supported the IRA and INLA in their role as 'freedom fighters', about three-quarters in their role as communal police and more than four-fifths in their role as communal defenders against attacks from nearby Protestants.[5] More generally support is likely to increase when the community feels under threat and to diminish sharply when 'their' side is responsible for some particularly horrific or mistaken killing. But communal solidarity and the fear of reprisals usually prevent what opposition there is from expressing itself openly.

Attitudes in the Protestant and Catholic communities as a whole, as opposed to these close-knit communities at the extremes, are also somewhat ambivalent and variable. Most opinion polls indicate that only a minority, typically less than 10 per cent of respondents in each community, are prepared to express any support for the use of paramilitary violence. This proportion also rises and falls in response to recent political and security developments.

And yet it seems that communal attitudes on what is and what is not acceptable have often acted as a restraining influence on the paramilitaries on both sides. There have been numerous occasions in the past twenty-five years when commentators were predicting that the level of violence was in the process of escalating into what could only be called civil war. But it has not as yet done so. After a series of particularly horrific incidents of multiple murder or indiscriminate bombing – most recently the IRA bomb on the Shankill Road and the retaliatory machine gun attack on a supposedly nationalist pub in Greysteel by loyalists – the paramilitaries have typically drawn back from further escalation or provocation and there has been a period of relative peace. Despite the ups and downs in popular views of the seriousness of 'the situation', the level of killing has remained remarkably stable over the years since the ending of internment in 1976 at between fifty and one hundred victims per year, as the figures in Table 3.1 indicate.

It does not follow that in the event of a serious deterioration in the security situation or a serious perceived threat to the essential interests of either community there would not be a substantial shift in attitudes and in the numbers of people prepared to join or give active support to 'their' defenders. This is what happened in the Catholic community in the aftermath of internment in 1971 and during the hunger strikes of 1981, and in the Protestant community following the suspension of the Stormont government in 1972, during the Ulster Workers Council Strike against the power-sharing government in 1974 and in the aftermath of the signing of the Anglo-Irish Agreement in 1985. Few doubt that it could happen again despite the evidence of increasing war-weariness on both sides.

The security response

The tactics and methods of the security forces in dealing with the various forms of public disorder and terrorist activity since 1968 have varied almost as much as those of the paramilitaries. In the initial years of the troubles a succession of mistakes in security policy made a major contribution to the escalation of the conflict. Since the mid-1970s they have generally achieved their basic objective of preventing the conflict from spiralling out of control.

The initial tactics of the Unionist government, the RUC and the B Specials during 1968 and 1969 in seeking to deal with the civil rights movement by banning demonstrations and by forceful confrontation of any disorders played into the hands of those who wanted to bring down the regime. When British soldiers eventually had to be deployed in August 1969 to relieve the RUC in Derry and prevent the spread of serious sectarian confrontations in Belfast, they acted and were accepted as an impartial peacekeeping force. But they were insufficiently trained in the necessary techniques and allowed themselves to be cast as the defenders of the status quo and as such to be drawn into conflict with the nationalist community, both in their response to widespread and repeated rioting and in dealing with the emerging IRA campaign. This culminated in the disastrous internment operation in August 1971 which was agreed to and carried out by the British Army largely to appease the Unionist government. In the period which followed, from August 1971 until the imposition of direct rule in March 1972, the Army was in effective control of security on the ground but was subject to conflicting pressures from the Unionist government in Belfast and the British government in London. During this period the number of casualties on all sides reached a peak, as shown in Table 3.1, and the Army was responsible for some of the most serious human rights violations that have occurred throughout the conflict, notably the systematic ill-treatment or torture of those arrested for interrogation and the shooting dead of thirteen civilians by paratroops in Derry on 'Bloody Sunday', 31 January 1972.

After the suspension of the Stormont government, the Army remained in control of security and was granted a fairly free hand in implementing the counter-insurgency policies which Brigadier Kitson and others had developed in the light of experience in Malaya and Aden. These involved mass arrests and screening of very large numbers of potential suspects and the internment without trial of all those suspected of terrorist activity. But the system proved only marginally more effective in stemming violence. It was eventually decided in 1975 that the military security strategy, which had been used primarily in nationalist areas, should be abandoned and that primacy in law enforcement in all areas should be restored to the police. Internment without trial was therefore phased out and increasing reliance was placed on the trial of suspected terrorists as criminals in special non-jury courts.

Since 1976, the RUC and the Army have worked more closely together on the implementation of this new policy. One important dimension has been a gradual shift in the respective numbers of soldiers and police, as shown in Table 3.2. At the height of the military security phase there were more than 16,500 British soldiers – for a brief period in 1973 over 23,000 – in Northern Ireland compared with some 4,500 full-time police officers, 2,500 part-time police reservists and 7,500 locally recruited and largely part-time soldiers of the Ulster Defence Regiment. By the end of the 1980s the number of soldiers from Britain had declined to around 10,000 and the number of local forces increased to 11,500 in the RUC – 8,500 full-time and 3,000 reserves – and 7,500 in the UDR (recently amalgamated into the Royal Irish Regiment). There are now some 20,000 locally recruited forces, or twice as many as are brought in from Britain. This has enabled substantial changes to be made in patterns of deployment and some substance to be given to the claim that the Army is acting only 'in aid of the civil power' as a back-up to the police. It also has significant political implications, as will be seen below, since more than 90 per cent of the police and almost all the members of what was the UDR are drawn from the Protestant community.

The different roles of the police and the regular Army and of the various special units within them and the way in which they are currently deployed can best be explained by distinguishing four major forms of action: regular preventive patrols, reactive deployment after incidents, intelligence work and preemptive action.

Regular patrols

The purpose of regular patrolling is partly to act as a deterrent, partly to collect information on the movement of suspects and any other suspicious activity and partly to demonstrate that the security forces are in control throughout Northern Ireland. The last of these is more significant than might be thought. If

Table 3.2 *Numbers in the Army, the UDR and the police 1972–92*

Year	British Army	Ulster Defence Regiment*	Royal Ulster Constabulary		Total
			Full-time	Reserves	
1972	17,000	8,500	4,250	1,250	31,000
1982	10,500	7,000	7,700	4,800	30,000
1992	12,000	5,500	8,500	4,500	30,500

*Amalgamated into the Royal Irish Regiment in 1992

Source: Official security statistics

it were not for regular patrols in certain nationalist and loyalist areas, the dominant paramilitary bodies would almost certainly seek to re-establish 'no-go' areas of the kind that were common in the early 1970s before the barricades were cleared in a massive show of military force – 'Operation Motorman' – in 1972. Some patrols are carried out on foot, others in police Land Rovers or equivalent Army vehicles. Many involve setting up temporary vehicle check points (VCPs) at which motorists are stopped and asked to produce some identification or to allow their vehicle to be searched in the hope of preventing the transport of arms and explosives and the delivery of car-bombs.

In some areas Army foot patrols still carry out regular personal searches and some basic questioning of young men and boys whom they come across. This is a carry-over from the military security policy under which very large numbers of people in nationalist areas were arrested and brought for questioning to the nearest Army barracks, in theory to establish their identity but in practice to gather intelligence on their lifestyle and associates and on paramilitary activity in the area. Extended 'screening' of this kind is now much less common.

But the frequency with which some young people in nationalist areas are still subjected to street searches and questioning and to verbal or physical abuse in the process is an issue of continuing controversy.[6] There is also controversy over the extent to which Army patrols and VCPs are accompanied by a police officer as a protection against unlawful or illegitimate conduct by soldiers. The Irish government secured a conditional undertaking to this effect from the British government on the signing of the Anglo-Irish Agreement in 1985. But there are still some country districts close to the border, notably in South Armagh and parts of Counties Tyrone and Fermanagh, in which the Army carries out regular patrols without a police presence and in which the policy of police primacy has apparently yet to be implemented.

Reactive deployment

The deployment of larger numbers in reaction to particular incidents such as a shooting attack, a bomb explosion or a riot is in a sense merely an extension of regular patrolling. Both the RUC and the Army must have sufficient numbers on call at any time to be able to clear and seal off relatively large areas as soon as they receive a bomb warning or in the aftermath of an explosion. It is also their practice to seal off relatively large areas surrounding any major shooting incident and to carry out systematic house searches in the vicinity in the hope of finding those responsible, their firearms or other relevant evidence. They must finally be able to react quickly, effectively and in sufficient strength to prevent any paramilitary body from asserting control in any area for any length of time. Though Army commanders accept that the IRA at least is able to assemble sufficient numbers in some areas to establish superior firepower for a time there can be no doubt that the Army could assemble overwhelming force in any part of

Northern Ireland at relatively short notice. This, in turn, makes it necessary to establish and to be able to defend separate or joint bases in strongly nationalist areas where the IRA has substantial communal support, such as West Belfast, Derry and South Armagh.

Whether the task of reactive deployment also requires the ring of heavily fortified border posts that have been established in recent years is more controversial. The Army presence in some border areas like South Armagh is highly visible both on the ground and in the air and can only be oppressive to many local residents. There is similar controversy over the policy of sealing off – or attempting to seal off – all border roads on which there is no permanent security post. The declared purpose of this is to prevent the flow of arms and explosives from IRA arms dumps in the Republic into Northern Ireland. There is no doubt that these dumps exist. The bulk of the 150 ton cargo of the Eksund and other consignments of arms from Libya in the mid-1980s is believed still to be hidden in caches south of the border. But it has been argued with some justification that it is quite impractical to seal such a long and tortuous border and that the inconvenience and unpopularity which the current policy causes to local residents, together with the risk it creates for soldiers deployed in isolated posts in hostile territory, far outweigh any practical security advantage. On this view, some at least of these border positions may have a greater political than security purpose.

Intelligence

The work of the police and the Army in anticipating and preventing terrorist attacks is less obvious but equally important. Most of this proactive role is carried out by specialized units – the RUC Special Branch, Army Intelligence, MI5 and the SAS. Intelligence is also obtained through cooperation with the Irish security forces. All this is highly secretive. But enough has been revealed in recent court cases and enquiries for a reasonably accurate picture to be given.[7]

The key to all work of this kind is accurate intelligence. In both Britain and Ireland it has traditionally been the task of a 'special branch' within the police to collect information and maintain files on subversive activity of all kinds, a role which dates back to the bombing campaign by the Fenians in the 1880s. But in Northern Ireland there has been a good deal of competition and rivalry between the police, military intelligence and the security services.

In the initial period of the current troubles the responsibility for intelligence was with the RUC Special Branch. Their information on IRA and other republican groups, which was relied on in selecting individuals for internment in 1971, however, proved to be inaccurate and out of date. As a result, during the period of military control from 1972 to 1975, the Army relied increasingly on its own intelligence, which it developed by using Brigadier Kitson's techniques of mass 'screening' of the population in nationalist areas and 'interrogation in depth' of selected suspects. Screening involved the compilation of information on the activities and associates of all active males by systematically arresting and questioning them and also on the normal occupancy of all houses by regular searches of houses, often on a door-to-door basis. Interrogation in depth initially involved the use of the so-called 'five techniques' of sensory deprivation – hooding, prolonged wall standing, restricted diet, deprivation of sleep, and constant noise – as a means of breaking down resistance to interrogation on the part of those thought to have valuable information on active terrorists. When these were publicly revealed and formally prohibited – they were later held to constitute inhuman and degrading treatment under the European Convention on Human Rights[8] – they were replaced by prolonged and 'robust' interrogation, often involving up to twenty lengthy sessions over a seven-day period. The information gleaned from these and other sources was then used by Army intelligence officers in selecting suspects for internment. Though few serious mistakes appear to have been made, the general public distaste for this military security system and the fact that it had clearly failed to eliminate the capacity of the IRA to continue its campaign eventually led to its abandonment.[9]

One of the major effects of the change in policy was to restore primary responsibility for interrogation and related intelligence gathering to the RUC Special Branch. Their objective was not simply to identify active terrorists with a view to internment without trial, but to obtain sufficient evidence to secure convictions against them in court. Some of the basic techniques were maintained, notably the prolonged questioning by relays of intelligence officers of suspects who were typically arrested at dawn in their own homes. But the system was reorganized on a planned basis. Two new police holding and interrogation centres were constructed at Castlereagh in Belfast and Gough Barracks in Armagh. And the emphasis of interrogation was shifted towards obtaining written or oral confessions which would be admissible in court. The political pressure to obtain convictions and the absence of effective safeguards, however, soon led to abuse. There were increasing complaints in 1977 and 1978 that confessions and admissions were being forced by systematic beating.[10] The government eventually intervened and imposed some reasonably effective safeguards – continuous supervision by uniformed officers through closed-circuit TV and stricter rules on such matters as the length of interrogation sessions, meal breaks and medical inspections.

The policy of the Special Branch then shifted towards obtaining convictions by relying on evidence from informers who could be persuaded to give evidence in court. Considerable efforts and resources were devoted to identifying and providing new lives in England or abroad for these potential witnesses and their families. This strategy of relying on 'supergrasses' as they were popularly referred to – the official description was 'reformed terrorists' – was initially successful in that more than 300 people belonging to or associated with the currently active terrorist groups were able to be charged, held in custody and in most cases convicted. In this period the level of terrorist activity declined significantly, as shown in Table 3.1. But almost all those involved were eventually released during 1985 when the judges reversed their initial readiness to convict on uncorroborated accomplice evidence. Future use of informer evidence was not completely ruled out. But the RUC was forced to abandon its 'supergrass strategy'.

The process of questioning is now directed towards the more usual mixture of attempting to persuade suspects to confess and obtaining more general intelligence on terrorist activity. In the early 1990s there was a renewed series of allegations of assault during interrogation at Castlereagh, some of which were accepted in court proceedings as well-founded. Public intervention by Amnesty International and complaints brought to the UN Committee on Torture by the Committee on the Administration of Justice, however, seem to have been effective in the sense that allegations of serious ill-treatment ceased.[11] The most significant continuing complaints are of verbal abuse and of repeated attempts by interrogators to recruit informers.

Pre-emptive action

The persistent search by special branch officers for informers is in practice directed as much to obtaining intelligence on future terrorist operations as to securing evidence which may permit convictions for past operations. One of the best methods of protecting potential victims, obtaining convictions or otherwise eliminating the threat from active terrorists, is to have advance information on planned attacks and to be able either to thwart them or to catch them in the act. Given the obvious difficulty and potential illegality of infiltrating members of the security forces into terrorist organizations, the most practical method is to recruit existing or potential future members as informers and to use them as a continuing source of intelligence. This policy enabled plans to be laid for the SAS and other specially trained units to lay ambushes with a view to arresting or more probably shooting dead IRA members on active service, since lethal shooting in such circumstances was relatively easy to justify or at least to defend in any legal proceedings. Ten lethal shootings of this kind were carried out in a short period during 1978. But three of the victims turned out to be wholly innocent and the public reaction appears to have led to a review of the strategy.

In the early 1980s, responsibility for acting on both military and police intelligence appears to have been passed to a specially trained police unit. But following a series of lethal shootings of a number of active but unarmed IRA and INLA members in 1982 this unit too was placed under a sustained legal and political spotlight. Three high-profile trials for murder were held and, though all the policemen charged were acquitted, sufficient was revealed of the underlying policy and of the close involvement of military intelligence to force the authorities to initiate the Stalker–Sampson inquiry into what became known as the 'shoot-to-kill' policy.[12] These developments appear to have prompted the restoration of responsibility for intercepting terrorists to the SAS and a more careful approach to the use of lethal force. But the number of active IRA members killed by undercover units in disputed circumstances remained relatively high. The most notorious incidents were the ambush and elimination of eight IRA men engaged in an attack on an unmanned police barracks in Loughgall in 1987 and of an IRA unit engaged in planning a bomb attack on a military band in Gibraltar in 1988.

Undercover operations of this kind have always been contro-

versial. There is a widespread view that some units in the
Army regard themselves as engaged in a war with the IRA in
which the elimination of the enemy by any means is fully
justified.[13] This is clearly contrary to the official government
position that the Army is acting only in aid of the police and
that all members of the security forces are subject to the
ordinary rule of law. A number of cases in which ordinary
soldiers have mistakenly shot civilians have resulted in prosecutions. But none of those involving undercover units since 1978
have yet come to court. Nor have any prosecutions been
initiated against those responsible for alleged abuses during
interrogation. This has prompted continuing concern that different rules are in practice applied to the work of intelligence and
undercover units compared with that of ordinary soldiers and
policemen.

The security forces as actors

This points to what may be the most significant conclusion
from this account of some of the ways in which the security
forces have responded to paramilitary violence over the past
twenty-five years, that each element in the security forces – the
uniformed police, the special branch, locally recruited soldiers
in what was the UDR, ordinary troops and intelligence and
undercover units in the Regular Army – has developed its own
methods of operation and its own internal rules on what is and
what is not permissible. Each is likely to react in a different
way to any major change in paramilitary tactics, in the law or
in the nature of the underlying political conflict. In his book
Low Intensity Operations, Brigadier Kitson set out his ideal of
total coordination in the fight against terrorism of all government agencies including the law. This has had some effect.
Since 1976 the government has sought to establish and maintain
decision-making structures which will lessen any institutional

conflict between the Army and the RUC in general and between military and police intelligence in particular. The reality remains that all the major elements in the security forces, like the paramilitaries they confront, are significant players in the conflict whose commitments and political influence will affect any eventual military or political outcome.

The legal framework

Some reference has already been made to the legal framework within which the security forces operate. Detailed discussion has deliberately been delayed until the essentials of security practice have been described, since in many respects the law has been tailored to comply with security requirements rather than the other way round. The extent to which the ordinary and emergency law which applies in Northern Ireland and the security practice which it authorizes meet both communal expectations and international standards is none the less an important practical and propaganda issue.

Under Unionist rule between 1921 and 1972 powers of internal security, which in practice meant the control of the IRA and other nationalist groups regarded as subversive, were regulated under the Civil Authorities (Special Powers) Acts. The Special Powers Act, as it was popularly known, gave the Minister of Home Affairs *carte blanche* to introduce internment without trial at any time and to make whatever other regulations he thought fit. The abuse of these powers, though they were used only occasionally, had always been one of the major complaints of nationalists and became a serious issue in the civil rights campaign in the late 1960s. The failure of the British legal system at the highest level to impose any effective limitation on their use in a case arising out of the banning of all 'Republican Clubs' in 1965 confirmed the view of nationalists that the Stormont government could do what it liked in this field.[14]

The Northern Ireland (Emergency Provisions) Act

When the Westminster government took direct control over security in March 1972 the replacement of the Special Powers Act was high on the agenda. But the new Northern Ireland (Emergency Provisions) Act enacted at Westminster in 1973 did little but change the names. The government had appointed a small committee of experts under Lord Diplock to review the law.[15] Lord Diplock limited his consultations to the security authorities and adopted, with only a few variations, a legal regime which would permit the Army to implement the kind of security policy recommended by Brigadier Kitson in *Low Intensity Operations*.

The military security system which was explicitly legalized under the 1973 Act had in practice been in operation since early in 1971. This kind of *ex post facto* legislation, as will be seen, has been a feature of security operations in Northern Ireland. A second important feature of emergency legislation is that once a power has been introduced it is rarely abandoned. Though the system of military security and internment without trial was kept in operation only until 1975, the power to reintroduce it at any time has been maintained by successive governments, despite repeated calls for it to be finally abandoned.

The most immediately significant aspect of the decision to restore police primacy in 1976 was that only those who could be convicted in a criminal court – or against whom criminal charges could plausibly be laid – could be put behind bars for any length of time. The Diplock Committee had identified two significant defects in the system which made convictions difficult to obtain: first, that confessions made during prolonged interrogation were inadmissible at common law on the ground that they could not be said to have been made voluntarily and without oppression; and second, that juries could not always be relied on to bring in verdicts in accordance with the evidence whether as a result of intimidation or partiality. Both these impediments were duly removed. The right to jury trial was abolished for 'scheduled offences' of a kind likely to be committed by terrorists. And all confessions were made admissible provided it could be shown that they had not been obtained by torture or inhuman or degrading treatment. Since 1973 this non-jury 'Diplock court' system has continued to operate in Northern Ireland as the primary means of dealing with terrorist suspects. Though there have been continuing complaints about undue reliance on uncorroborated confessions and, during the period of the 'supergrass system', on the uncorroborated evidence of accomplices, Diplock courts in themselves have perhaps been the least controversial aspect of the security system.[16]

The Prevention of Terrorism Act

The final significant elements in the emergency security regime were introduced in 1974 under the Prevention of Terrorism (Temporary Provisions) Act which was rushed through Parliament after the Birmingham pub bombs. This was directed primarily against the extension of the IRA campaign to Britain and provided for the exclusion of anyone suspected of involvement in terrorism from Great Britain to Northern Ireland or to the Republic of Ireland. It also authorized detention for questioning for up to seven days, compared with the 72 hours allowed under the Northern Ireland (Emergency Provisions) Act. These powers of arrest and exclusion from Great Britain have been widely used against members of the Irish community in Great Britain and also as a means of preventing anyone directly or indirectly concerned with the republican movement from entering the country. The corresponding power to exclude from Northern Ireland has very rarely been used.

Since 1974 very few significant changes have been made in
these emergency powers. The authorities have accepted that
there is a need for a regular independent review of the legislation and when it has periodically been renewed or re-enacted a
few amendments have been accepted, for example, to tighten
the grounds on which arrests may be made and searches
carried out. But the essentials of the structures put in place in
1973 and 1974 have not been changed. The most significant
alterations have not been to limit or restrict police or Army
powers but to increase them whenever that has been demanded
by the security authorities. In the review of the legislation prior
to its re-enactment in 1989, for example, Lord Colville recommended the introduction of a number of significant limitations
and safeguards, including the removal of the power to reintroduce internment and the video-recording of police interroga-
tions, and a few extensions, such as a new power to search
documents.[17] None of the limitations or safeguards were accepted and all the extensions were approved.

There has been a similar reaction to recommendations for
changes in other related laws. In 1988, in the aftermath of
some IRA atrocities, pressure from the security authorities to
limit the right to silence by allowing adverse inferences to be
drawn in certain cases where the defendant has given no
explanation either under police interrogation or in court was
accepted and the Criminal Evidence (Northern Ireland) Order
was rushed through Parliament without any opportunity for
serious debate or amendment. At the same time Sinn Féin and
other groups were banned from television and radio. Objections
from the security forces have also blocked any action on the
recommendations by Lord Colville and others for the amendment of the law on the use of lethal force with a view to
providing a more workable range of sanctions to deal with the
misuse of lethal force by soldiers and policemen. Of the eighteen prosecutions initiated in such cases since 1982, all but three
have resulted in acquittals. Finally, the government has insisted

on retaining the power to interrogate suspects for up to seven days without judicial authority. Though the European Court of Human Rights ruled that the power contravened the European Convention on Human Rights, the government's response was immediately to derogate from the relevant provision of the Convention.[18]

It is hard to resist the conclusion that it is often the views of the security authorities on what should be permitted under emergency and related legislation that determine the law rather than the law that sets effective limits on what the security forces are permitted to do.

The human rights dimension

The extent to which the parties to any internal conflict can be shown to have broken international human rights standards is now an important factor in the eventual outcome. Allegations of human rights abuses are a powerful weapon in the propaganda war which is an integral part of most political or constitutional conflicts of this kind and may have a significant impact on the pressure or support from other countries on the responsible government.

Northern Ireland is no exception. Since 1969 there has been a long succession of reports by reputable human rights organizations, such as the locally based Committee on the Administration of Justice, Amnesty International and more recently Human Rights Watch and the Lawyers Committee on Human Rights, drawing attention to serious human rights abuses in Northern Ireland. Cases from Northern Ireland have also been prominent in the workload of the European Commission and Court of Human Rights. As might be expected, these allegations and reports have been widely publicized by Sinn Féin and its supporters at home and abroad in promoting their campaign against the continuing 'British presence' in Ireland. International attention has more recently been focused by the British government and many others on the long succession of 'terrorist atrocities' carried out by the IRA and other paramilitary organizations. Is there anything to choose between these conflicting claims? Has either side secured any practical advantage in the war of words? Or are human rights abuses on all sides only to be expected in an armed conflict that has been sustained for twenty-five years?

The list of abuses alleged against the security forces cannot be dismissed as occasional malpractice by individual soldiers or policemen. From early in 1970 there were complaints of widespread and uncontrolled harassment and assaults by soldiers patrolling in nationalist areas. The mass internment operation of August 1971 was followed by numerous complaints of systematic brutality and ill-treatment against many of those arrested and preplanned ill-treatment or torture against those chosen for interrogation in depth. Since then there have been continuing complaints of systematic abuse on a wide range of matters: the deliberate use of lethal force against suspected terrorists by undercover Army and police units, resulting in more than 100 unjustified killings; the inadequacy of inquest procedures; the uncontrolled use of more than one hundred thousand rounds of potentially lethal rubber and plastic bullets, causing fifteen deaths during riots and confrontations in nationalist areas and one in a loyalist area; the repeated arrest and questioning for intelligence gathering of large numbers of people against whom there cannot have been any real suspicion of unlawful activity; lengthy periods during which assaults and other ill-treatment of suspects detained for prolonged interrogation at Castlereagh and Gough holding centres became standard practice; reliance on forced confessions obtained during prolonged interrogation and on untrustworthy evidence from supergrasses as the sole basis for convictions in non-jury special courts; and the refusal to segregate or grant special status to politically motivated offenders in prison and the unjustified penalization of those who refused to accept the status of ordinary criminals. In Britain itself there has been a succession of appalling miscarriages of justice in cases arising from the conflict in Northern Ireland and continuing allegations of the misuse of the arrest powers under the Prevention of Terrorism Act.

The British judicial and constitutional system has proved itself to be singularly ill-equipped to deal with these widely felt concerns and allegations. The absence of any entrenched rights under the unwritten British constitution and the fact that some of the contested practices have been directly or indirectly authorized by Parliament have made it difficult for the courts to intervene, even if they had wished to do so. In practice the judges have been reluctant to search for grounds on which they might intervene to prevent or punish malpractice by the security forces on the general ground that decisions on matters of national security must be left to the Executive. When judges in the lower courts have ruled against the authorities, as the judges in Northern Ireland have done in some cases, the House of Lords in London has invariably overruled them. Parliament has been equally ineffective. The general approach of most MPs has been to give the benefit of any doubt to the security forces in dealing with what by any standards is a concerted and threatening terrorist campaign. When public concern expressed through television, newspapers or otherwise has demanded that some action be taken to deal with serious abuses, the response of the government has typically been to appoint an official inquiry with terms of reference limited to making recommendations for alterations in law or practice for the future rather than to ensure a remedy for past abuses.[19] More recently the tendency has been to appoint semi-permanent commissioners to review or report on matters of concern, often on a non-statutory basis, but without any powers of adjudication or enforcement.[20] Though in many cases the fact that abuses may have occurred has been tacitly recognized by the informal settlement of claims for compensation by the victims, this has very rarely been extended to include any formal action to punish those responsible. This is especially true in cases where undercover operations by the security services or the Army have been involved. Many independent observers and most of the nationalist community in Northern Ireland remain unconvinced that the British authorities are willing to permit any rigorous and independent scrutiny or adjudication on the activities of the security forces in Northern Ireland.

International remedies

Dissatisfaction with the response to allegations of human rights abuses at national level soon led to an increasing number of cases being referred for international adjudication under the European Convention on Human Rights. But here too the response has been somewhat equivocal. Decisions have been made against the United Kingdom in respect of the ill-treatment of suspects during interrogation in 1971[21] and the operation of seven-day detention for interrogation in 1987.[22] But in many other cases the complaints have been rejected and the authorities have been at least partially vindicated. The use of internment without trial in 1971,[23] a killing by the use of plastic bullets for riot control in 1976,[24] the refusal of concessions to convicted IRA prisoners demanding special status in prison in 1980,[25] the use of lethal force against suspected terrorists attempting to drive through a roadblock in 1985[26] and the entry of a derogation to legitimize the continuation of seven-day detention following the previous Court decision against it[27] have all been approved by the Commission or the Court at Strasbourg. In all these cases both the Commission and the Court have in practice been ready to grant the government a wide 'margin of appreciation' – i.e. to give the government the benefit of any doubt – in adopting the special measures it thinks appropriate in dealing with terrorism and associated disorders. The recent decisions of the European Commission and Court on the minimum acceptable European standard in matters of this kind have certainly been insufficiently demanding to convince many in the nationalist community in Northern Ireland and in the international human rights community that no further action is needed to control abuse. Reducing the widespread feeling of alienation from the law enforcement system among the nationalist community will require the implementation and monitoring of rather more demanding standards. Some of the possibilities are discussed in the final chapters of this book.

Human rights abuses by paramilitaries

The list of systematic human rights violations alleged against the IRA and other paramilitary bodies is also lengthy. Even if it were accepted that their members are entitled to use armed force against members of the security forces, many of their regular practices are clearly contrary to international standards: the assassination of politicians, civilians and probably also off-duty part-time soldiers, bomb attacks on civilians, the summary execution of suspected informers, the beating and kneecapping of persons suspected of anti-social practices and many other forms of attack designed to terrify the population at large are all unlawful under either customary international law or international humanitarian law under the Geneva Conventions and Protocols. Dealing with these allegations, however, raises difficult issues. Until recently most international organizations were unwilling to monitor and report on alleged human rights violations by non-state bodies on the ground that only states were subject to international human rights law. A number of leading human rights organizations, including Amnesty International and Human Rights Watch, have now abandoned this position and are beginning to monitor and report on violations by organized non-state bodies.[28] As yet there are no permanent international bodies or agencies with the right to make formal rulings on matters of this kind. But it seems right that the practices of organized movements like the IRA, which purports to be fighting on behalf of the general population in the pursuit of self-determination and democracy, should be subjected to the same international scrutiny as the state forces they oppose and that their political representatives should be held responsible for clear violations in a similar way to the governments of states. None of the rules of international human rights or humanitarian law are in practice enforceable against states which choose to ignore them. The fact that they cannot be enforced against non-state bodies either is not a good reason for refraining from any attempt to judge their actions by the same rules.

A sustainable conflict?

One way to end this chapter would be to attempt an assessment on who has won the conflict.

The simple answer to such a question would be that both sides now accept they cannot win a military victory. Senior British Army officers have for some time been willing to state openly that the war against the IRA cannot be won by any methods which would be politically acceptable. Until recently the IRA leadership also appeared to be resigned to an indefinite continuation of their struggle. Talk about 'one last push' has become much less frequent than talk about the need to maintain a war of attrition until the British government or people finally decide that it is not worth continuing.

A more realistic way of approaching the question of winning and losing may be to ask it in respect of the more limited objectives which both sides now accept. The British Army and the police in Northern Ireland now appear to have moved towards a strategy of containment pending the achievement of some form of political accommodation. And, despite the occasional upsurge of bombings and sectarian killings, it seems likely that they will be able to carry out that strategy indefinitely. The IRA appear to have set themselves the limited objective of an indefinite continuation of something like their present level of operation in the hope that that will be enough to secure an eventual British withdrawal, not least by a government more sympathetic to Irish unification than the current Conservative government. Seen in these terms, both sides appear to have the capacity to continue indefinitely.

The impact of the conflict

A better way to conclude may be to attempt an assessment of the impact of a continuation of military conflict on the kind of political accommodation which may ultimately be achievable.

The starting point must be the paradox with which the chapter began – that many people in Northern Ireland go about their business as if the conflict was inevitable or was happening somewhere else. Daily life for most families goes on more or less as it does anywhere else in Britain or Ireland. The children go to school and take their examinations in the summer. Young people go to cinemas, pubs and pop concerts. Adults go to work and those that are unemployed fill their time in the same way as their counterparts in depressed areas in the rest of Britain and Ireland. The better-off have dinner parties and go to concerts and restaurants like their counterparts everywhere else.

One striking way of getting this sense of normality across to those who have not experienced ordinary life in Northern Ireland is to compare the deaths, injuries and inconvenience caused by the conflict with those caused by road accidents and other ordinary accidents and disasters. The comparative figures

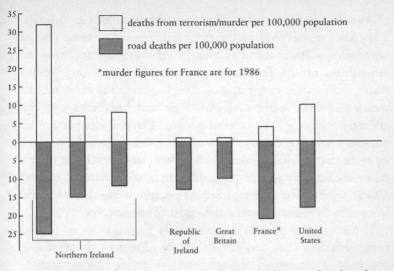

Figure 3.1 *The risk of sudden death in Northern Ireland and some other countries. (The bar dates: NI, 1972, 1981, 1991; murder figures for France, 1986; all the rest, 1991)*

in Figure 3.1 show that life in Northern Ireland is a good deal safer than in many other places in Europe and North America. The level of deaths and serious injuries in Northern Ireland from the continuing conflict is currently about half the level of death and serious injury from traffic accidents. And though the combined level of deaths from the conflict and road accidents is considerably higher than that for all murders and road accidents in Britain and the Republic of Ireland, where road deaths are only slightly higher, they are considerably less than in France and the United States, where road deaths and murders respectively are very much higher. A holiday in Northern Ireland for a Frenchman or an American is a good deal less risky than staying at home. And most people in Northern Ireland have less direct contact with death or injury from the conflict than from ordinary accidents.

Comparative statistics like these, of course, are no consolation to the families of those who have been killed or injured. They take no account of the traumatic nature of most deaths and injuries from terrorist attacks, the intense suffering of individuals or the fears and antagonisms which they create throughout whole communities. And they conceal the extent to which the daily reports of shootings and bombings and the lasting evidence of the conflict provided by the destruction of buildings and large sections of town centres affect the perceptions of the whole population. But they are a reminder of the relatively small impact of the conflict in terms of direct personal loss or injury. The vast majority of people in Northern Ireland live perfectly normal lives in the midst of the conflict.

The impact of the conflict in purely financial terms is also somewhat less than might be thought. Most of those whose property or businesses are attacked are entitled to compensation at public expense. Though there are repeated complaints over the bureaucracy and delay involved in the compensation system, most victims receive a relatively satisfactory settlement. Some derive a considerable windfall benefit from being able to dispose of marginal or failing businesses or unsaleable stock at favourable prices. And there are, of course, some cases in which inflated or fraudulent claims are made and probably a few in which paramilitaries are contracted to destroy property or businesses with a view to extracting and sharing in compensation from the government. The construction industry also benefits from the regular flow of work on the renovation or renewal of the premises affected. All this, including the well-paid official employment and private legal fees and expenses generated by the system, is ultimately paid for not by insurance premiums but by the British taxpayer as part of the general subvention to public expenditure in Northern Ireland. The total subvention in recent years, as will be seen, has been some £3,000 million per year. The impact of the conflict on the local economy is thus, in Keynesian terms, beneficial rather than malign. The longer-term ill-effects in terms of the difficulty in

attracting new investment are felt not so much by the established business community as by those who suffer unemployment as a result of the general stagnation of the industrial and
commercial sectors.

Pressures for peace

The most accurate final conclusion may be that the conflict in
Northern Ireland is not currently hurting anyone enough to
affect the capacity on all sides to continue indefinitely. It does
not follow, of course, that if it was hurting more, the communal
reaction would not be to raise the intensity of the conflict
rather than to seek a peaceful compromise. Experience in other
communal or ethnic conflicts, like those in Cyprus, Lebanon
and Yugoslavia, does not indicate that the propensity to compromise always increases as the situation deteriorates.

It is none the less true that everyone involved has suffered
significant losses both in terms of casualties and otherwise.
There is a palpable sense of war-weariness on all sides. The
Unionist community, particularly those associated with the
security forces, have experienced twenty-five years of death
and destruction and the gradual erosion of their political
confidence. The IRA campaign has inflicted equally heavy
costs on its own community and has caused a degree of
communal separation and antagonism which has made its
ultimate goal of unification even less credible. The British
government has had to pay the heavy financial costs of all
aspects of the conflict and has faced considerable international
criticism of its actions in Northern Ireland. And the British
people too have suffered both the trauma of atrocities like the
Birmingham and Warrington bombs and the more mundane
but widespread disruption of public transport in London and
elsewhere. No one can avoid counting the cost of an indefinite
continuation of the conflict. The prospect that there might be

another twenty years of armed struggle without any certainty of ultimate success has clearly played a part in persuading the British government to open channels of contact with the IRA and some IRA leaders to pursue the possibility of a negotiated settlement.

CHAPTER 4

The Peacemakers

Like most other areas of intercommunal conflict Northern Ireland has generated a succession of peacemakers, both from within and abroad. Some of these have hit the headlines, like the Nobel Prize-winning Peace People in the mid-1970s and more recently Initiative '92 and the Opsahl Commission in 1993. Others have worked more quietly behind the scenes in local communities. Some, like the churches and the British and Irish governments, have had peacemaking thrust upon them. Yet for many years none appeared to have made much lasting impact on the continuing conflict. In a decade in which major successes in making peace have been achieved in some of the most intractable conflicts in other places, notably in Germany, in South Africa and in Palestine, why did the peacemakers in Northern Ireland apparently make so little progress? Was it a failure of technique? Or is the nature of the conflict even more intractable? And what are the prospects for the success of the current search for peace following the Hume–Adams talks and the Downing Street Declaration?

The main burden of seeking an accommodation between the two communities and their political representatives has naturally fallen on the British and Irish governments. They have cooperated in a long succession of failed initiatives, notably the Sunningdale Agreement of 1973 and the power-sharing government which it launched and the Anglo-Irish Agreement of 1985. To understand the background to the current search for peace and a lasting political settlement the story of those initiatives and the reasons why they failed needs to be told.

And what of the less formal attempts at peacemaking by the churches and other voluntary organizations – what have they achieved in reducing the scale of the conflict and suffering even if they have not solved the problem?

The churches – peacemakers or part of the problem?

After every serious escalation in paramilitary violence the leaders of the main churches in Northern Ireland – Cardinal Cathal Daly for the Roman Catholic Church, Archbishop Robin Eames for the Church of Ireland, the Moderator of the Presbyterian Church and the President of the Methodist Church in Ireland – typically issue individual or joint statements condemning the perpetrators and reaffirming their commitment to the Christian values of peace, tolerance and forgiveness. They often join in prayers for peace and in appeals to political leaders for compromise and have made many trips to the United States and other countries where they feel there may be some misunderstanding on the nature of the conflict or on the legitimacy of the violence. Yet the popular perception remains that the conflict is at least in part a religious one between Protestants and Catholics. Are the churches really peacemakers or are they part of the problem?

There can be no doubt that the church leaders and all but a few ordinary priests and ministers are sincere in their condemnations of violence and in their prayers for peace – provided it is on their terms. There has also been considerable progress in developing interchurch contacts between Protestants and Catholics both among church leaders and at local level in shared services and other cross-communal initiatives.[1] An outstanding example of a Christian programme for reconciliation has been the long-established Corrymeela Community in Belfast and Ballycastle.[2] It is now much less common than it would have been in the 1960s and before to find local Catholic priests who refuse to attend a Protestant service or Protestant ministers who refuse to attend a Catholic service. The attitude on both sides to mixed marriages is much more relaxed, not least in respect of the previously strict rule that the Catholic partner should be required to promise that any children will be brought up as Catholics. More recently, all the main churches have agreed the content of a common syllabus for religious education for the new Northern Ireland Curriculum.[3]

These indications of a greater readiness to work together and to recognize the sincerity of other forms of Christianity, however, have not made much impact on the underlying pressure within each church both to retain the allegiance of its members and to reflect their views on matters of public concern.

The worry over losing control over 'their' people is clearly apparent in the churches' approach to integrated education. None of the churches has played an active role in the development of integrated schools, which are usually regarded as more of a threat to established schools under the control of or closely attached to the various churches than as a means of increasing contact and mutual respect between the two communities. The Catholic Church initially refused to give First Communion to children who attended integrated schools, though in the face of widespread public criticism this stance was abandoned. But it still refuses to appoint chaplains to carry out denominational instruction in any integrated school or to nominate members of boards of governors for controlled integrated schools as the legislation provides. And it regularly advises parents to send their children to Catholic rather than integrated or state schools. The Protestant churches have been less openly hostile, but they have not given much encouragement to the development of new integrated schools or to the conversion of existing schools to integrated status.[4]

The close connection between the churches and the political

positions and aspirations of their congregations is also immediately apparent in many of the public statements of their leaders. The Catholic bishops regularly add to their condemnations of IRA violence some expression of their concern on behalf of the Catholic community over alleged breaches of law and human rights by members of the security forces. Protestant bishops and ministers regularly add to their condemnations of loyalist violence some reference to the feelings of the Protestant community over the threat to their position from militant nationalism. The political leanings of some leading members of both the Roman Catholic and the Protestant churches are also well known to all. The Catholic Primate during most of the 1970s and 1980s, Cardinal Tomas O Fiacch, frequently expressed his personal commitment to the ideal of a united Ireland. A number of elected representatives of the main unionist parties are active ministers in their respective churches. The Rev. Ian Paisley is as well known for his militant unionism as for his militant anti-Catholic views.[5] And there are two other Protestant ministers who are currently MPs, the Rev. Martin Smyth of the Official Unionists and the Rev. William McCrea of the Democratic Unionists; another, the Rev. Robert Bradford, was assassinated by the IRA in 1981. At a lower level, there is evidence that Catholic priests are less willing to consider compromise and accommodation than most other groups in Northern Ireland.[6] And the Union Jack has a prominent place in many Protestant churches. In this way members of both communities and the in betweens are regularly reminded that their churches are involved in and share their political as well as their religious differences.

This involvement and lack of impartiality make it difficult for the church leaders to play a major role in the search for a settlement to the conflict. In the political sphere they are inevitably subordinate to elected political representatives. A few church leaders on the Protestant side have been involved in sporadic confidential talks with the IRA and loyalist paramilitaries in an attempt to persuade them that their campaigns are futile. A few Catholic priests have also become deeply involved in attempting to dissuade the IRA from certain forms of activity, notably during the hunger strikes in 1981 and in laying the foundations for the current peace process. But the most common form of peacemaking by the churches – their regular denunciations of violence and their occasional calls for political compromise and accommodation – have had little observable impact. Fundamentally, the churches are more interested in tending and representing the interests of their adherents than in serious action in pursuit of a larger accommodation.

People power

In recent years the involvement of large numbers of ordinary people in public meetings and demonstrations has played a part in the resolution of seemingly intractable political conflicts such as the unification of Germany and the democratization of the Philippines. There have been some examples of the mobilization of people power in the pursuit of peace in Northern Ireland. But none has as yet had as much practical impact as the mobilization of ordinary people in support of communal rather than cross-communal objectives. Does this mean that the 'people' in Northern Ireland are less interested in peace than in protecting the interests of their own communities? The answer is, of course, that the people are divided and open to influence on this, as on other matters, and that there is scope for mobilization for many different objectives.

In the initial stages of the current round of conflict in 1968 and 1969, large numbers of people, mostly Catholic but with a significant admixture of Protestants and unaligned, were involved in peaceful demonstrations in support of civil rights objectives. The counter-demonstrations by large numbers of loyalists led by the Rev. Ian Paisley and others and the confrontational tactics adopted by the police, however, had the effect of turning what began as peaceful cross-communal action into an almost exclusively Catholic campaign of street protests which often developed into rioting.[7] Popular action within the Protestant community in this period, notably the mass mobilization of many thousands of men in military-style parades by the Ulster Defence Association (UDA) in 1972 following the imposition of direct rule, was likewise directed exclusively to the assertion of communal rather than cross-communal concerns.

The first major break in this pattern was the sudden emergence of the Peace People in May 1976.[8] The movement was launched as a protest at the deaths of two children who were run down when a car being used by an IRA unit in an attack on the security forces went out of control in West Belfast. The prime movers were Mairead Maguire, the children's aunt, and Betty Williams, a community worker from a Protestant area. The initial peace marches in Belfast and Derry attracted huge crowds from both communities, and a widely representative organizing committee with a preponderance of women was soon formed. Large sums of money were raised from supporters abroad and in 1977 the Nobel Peace Prize was awarded to Mairead Maguire and Betty Williams. But the succession of marches appeared to have little impact on the activities of the paramilitaries, whose campaigns of shootings and bombings continued unabated. And when an attempt was made to develop a more overtly political agenda, which included a claim to replace the established political parties with an 'assembly of the Peace People', the level of popular support declined rapidly. Though the Peace People continue to operate, they have abandoned the strategy of mass demonstrations and now concentrate on lower-profile activities such as assisting those who want to make a break from involvement in paramilitary organizations.

There have been a number of other attempts to generate popular pressure against the continuing paramilitary violence.

In 1970, Women Together was founded by Ruth Agnew and Monica Patterson to promote peace and reconciliation in Northern Ireland. The trade unions have sponsored a number of well-supported demonstrations against particular acts of violence, such as attacks by the IRA on construction workers involved in contacts for the security forces and attacks by loyalists on individual Catholic workers. In 1989, the Peace Train movement initiated what has become an annual North–South demonstration against the continuing disruption by the IRA of travel links between Belfast and Dublin. In 1990, Families against Intimidation and Terrorism was formed to protest against the intimidation by the IRA and others of those alleged to be involved in anti-social activity in nationalist areas. In 1993, the surge of popular outrage in the Republic against terrorist attacks by the IRA in Britain, sparked by the killing of two young children by a shopping precinct bomb in Warrington, led to the formation of a new Dublin-based peace campaign and the Warrington Project, designed to increase understanding between the people of both islands. All these and many other similar initiatives have made a major if brief impact in television, radio and press coverage of events in Northern Ireland and make a continuing contribution to better understanding of the nature of the conflict. But none has been able to generate and sustain the level of popular support that was apparent in the weekly marches in Leipzig in 1989 or the mass protests against the Marcos regime in Manila in 1984. And none has had any more observable impact on the level or nature of paramilitary violence than the original Peace People movement in 1976.

It is difficult to pinpoint the reasons for this lack of impact. One possibility is that underground paramilitary organizations are less susceptible to popular influence even than dictatorial governments. Another is that the numbers involved in peace demonstrations, except perhaps those initiated by the Peace People in 1976, have been too small to mark anything like an overwhelming popular desire for change. The numbers ready to turn out for peace demonstrations in recent years have certainly been many fewer than those who have been ready to join in demonstrations of communal solidarity, such as the funerals of the IRA and INLA hunger strikers in 1981 or the massive popular protest against the Anglo-Irish Agreement in November 1985, for which estimates varied between 100,0000 and 200,000. Or it may be that too many people in Northern Ireland have become resigned to, or are isolated from, the continuing violence to be bothered to turn out to express their opposition to it in this way.

Community relations projects

Whatever the reasons for the failure of large-scale peace movements, the main focus of voluntary peacemaking groups in Northern Ireland since the 1970s has been on relatively small-scale initiatives designed to improve relations between the two communities at a local level. There has been a huge range of projects, some supported exclusively by voluntary fund raising and some by a mixture of voluntary and governmental grants.

Most of the projects have focused on encouraging contacts between members of different communities. Many British and foreign churches and charities have organized or supported schemes for children or families from deprived or 'front line' areas from both communities to share outings or longer holidays together. Initially, many of these schemes involved trips to Britain, other European countries or America where those involved were encouraged to discuss their differences more openly. But it has been reported that any benefit in terms of greater understanding or personal friendships across the communal divide was usually limited to the period of the trip and was not continued when those involved went back home. In some cases more ambitious projects were developed in

which leading members of opposing communities were involved
in structured group discussions aimed at exposing and eliminating deeper antagonisms and misunderstandings. But these too
seemed to have little positive impact in reducing the different
attitudes and aspirations on either side. It may not be very far
from the truth to say, as some cynical commentators put it,
that most people in Northern Ireland understand each other
very well; it does not follow that they must therefore agree
with each other.

Another focus of many voluntary and state-aided projects
has been on creating more lasting structures in which members
of both communities may cooperate on matters of shared
interest, such as planning decisions and job-creation projects.
This was one of the objectives of the community development
programme initiated by the Community Relations Commission
in 1969 and carried on by local district councils when the
Commission was abolished in 1974. One of the best examples
of this kind of action has been the creation of the Greater West
Belfast Community Council on which representatives from
some of the most exclusively nationalist and loyalist areas can
discuss their immediate problems and seek mutually acceptable
solutions. More recently the government has agreed to reconsti-
tute a more general Community Relations Council with the
task of encouraging and funding cross-communal projects of
all kinds, from training workshops on community relations,
anti-intimidation programmes and the development of integrated schools to local history societies and local cultural
festivals. A recent development in Dungannon, for example, is
the creation of a local committee with the specific objective of
developing and maintaining integrated housing by countering
and guarding against the kind of intimidation and fear described above. The promotion of what have become popularly
known as the 'two traditions' in all forms of cultural and
artistic activity has also been one of the major objectives of the
new Council.[10] There is now a huge range of local projects and

bodies of all kinds with some cross-communal objectives or membership and a substantial amount of governmental and charitable money is spent on them.

There are also a number of significant voluntary initiatives whose objective is to improve communications and understanding between people and organizations on both sides of the border. The best known is Co-operation North, which has developed a wide range of cross-border programmes in education, community contacts, sport and commerce. Many such projects are supported by the official intergovernmental body, the International Fund for Ireland, and by the independent Ireland Fund.[11]

It is difficult to assess the practical effect of these initiatives. Most funding agencies, both governmental and charitable, appear to regard evidence of active participation by members of both communities, as opposed to evidence that the project has in some way reduced or counteracted the pressures towards communal separation, as sufficient in itself to justify continued support.[12] But the numbers involved in many of these projects are relatively small, and many of those are often better regarded as people in between the two communities than as committed to one or another.[13] There is no clear evidence that twenty years of community relations work has increased the proportion of people who regard themselves as a bridge between the communities or reduced the trend towards greater separation. An alternative justification might be that some at least of the projects have increased the level of mutual acceptance and respect between members of the two communities. Even if this is true, however, it has not as yet resulted in any greater readiness on the part of their political leaders to enter into a general political settlement. Whether the continuing community relations work and the latest and most ambitious project of this kind – Initiative '92 and the Opsahl Commission – will prove more effective in securing acceptance of the current peace initiative by the British and Irish governments remains to be seen. But first the story of earlier governmental attempts at peacemaking must be told.

The British–Irish search for peace and stability

The initial response of the British government at a political level to the renewed outbreak of communal conflict in 1968 was limited to putting pressure on the incumbent and exclusively Unionist administration to eliminate all forms of discrimination against Catholics.[14] When the deteriorating security situation led to the imposition of 'direct rule' from London in 1972, this policy was extended to include the creation of a devolved government which would contain elected representatives from both communities. During 1973 this policy was pursued with the cooperation of the Irish government and resulted in the Sunningdale Agreement which was signed in December 1973 by the two governments and representatives of the Unionist, Alliance and Social Democratic and Labour Parties from Northern Ireland. The Agreement contained four major elements: a statement of the aspiration of the Irish government and the SDLP for the unification of Ireland together with a formal declaration of what has become known as the consent principle, that 'there could be no change in the status of Northern Ireland until a majority of the people in Northern Ireland desired a change in that status'; a proposal that a Council of Ireland, comprising a joint North–South ministerial council and a consultative assembly of equal numbers of elected representatives from North and South, should be established to deal with certain economic, environmental and security matters; an agreement that Northern Ireland would be governed by a 'power-sharing' executive composed of members of the three participating parties, as had already been agreed in internal talks within Northern Ireland; and an agreement that there should be greater cooperation in the fight against terrorism on both sides of the border.

It did not prove possible, however, to implement this elaborate package. A new 'power-sharing' executive was established in January 1974. But there were continuing difficulties over the proposal for the Council of Ireland in the light of the widespread opposition to it in the unionist community, led by the Rev. Ian Paisley and others who had refused to participate in the Sunningdale Agreement or in any form of power-sharing. Opponents of the Agreement were elected in eleven of the twelve Northern Ireland constituencies in the British general election of February 1974. The executive was eventually brought down in May 1974 by a political strike by Protestant workers which the authorities failed to contain and which ultimately generated sufficient momentum to paralyse economic activity throughout Northern Ireland. The government in the Republic also encountered legal difficulties over its purported recognition of the status of Northern Ireland: in a test case brought by opponents of the Sunningdale Agreement in the Republic, the Irish judges held that while the declaration in the Agreement was merely a statement of policy, any attempt to give practical effect to it might be unconstitutional, given the assertion of jurisdiction over Northern Ireland in Articles 2 and 3 of the Irish Constitution of 1937.

Following the collapse of the Sunningdale package the new Labour government in Britain made a further attempt to get the local political parties to agree on new structures for devolved self-government. In May 1975, elections were held for a Northern Ireland Constitutional Convention with the task of preparing new proposals for devolved government. But the unionist and nationalist parties could not agree. The unionist parties proposed that power should be shared only at the level of supervisory parliamentary committees and failed to make any provision for an 'Irish dimension'. But the SDLP refused to accept any such package. The Labour Government then abandoned its efforts to achieve a compromise and for the remainder of the 1970s fell back on a strategy of what was intended to be benevolent and impartial rule from London.

The Anglo-Irish Agreement

In the 1980s both the British and the Irish governments committed themselves more openly and explicitly to a policy of recognizing and accommodating the existence of two separate communities. The process began with two summit meetings in 1980 between the British Prime Minister, Mrs Thatcher, and the Irish Taoiseach, Charles Haughey, at which it was agreed that 'the totality of the relationships' on the islands of Britain and Ireland should be explored in a series of joint intergovernmental studies. It culminated in the Anglo-Irish Agreement signed at Hillsborough in Northern Ireland on 15 November 1985. This contained four principal elements. The first was a reiteration of the consent principle in a joint declaration that 'any change in the status of Northern Ireland would only come about with the consent of a majority of the people of Northern Ireland'; this was linked to an undertaking by the British government to give effect to the unification of Ireland if and when a majority of the people of Northern Ireland formally consent to it. The second was the creation of an intergovernmental ministerial conference, jointly chaired by British and Irish ministers and backed by a permanent secretariat at Maryfield in Belfast, with the primary task of seeking agreement on measures which would recognize and accommodate the interests of the two communities in Northern Ireland. The third was agreement on a policy of devolving power to a Northern Ireland administration provided it secured the cooperation of representatives of both communities. And the fourth was agreement that cross-border cooperation on security and economic and social matters should be continued and enhanced.

This formal declaration of cooperation and unity of purpose by the two governments was widely welcomed in Britain and the Republic of Ireland and by other countries, notably the United States, with an interest in resolving the conflict in

Northern Ireland. But there was significant opposition both from traditional republicans on both sides of the border and especially from unionists in Northern Ireland.

Both Sinn Féin and Fianna Fáil, the largest political party in the Republic, expressed their concern over the implications of the Agreement for Articles 2 and 3 of the Irish Constitution, which assert jurisdiction over the whole of Ireland. But Fianna Fáil opposition was mainly formal and was not reflected in opinion polls or other popular reaction. When Fianna Fáil won an election in the Republic in the following year, it found no difficulty in continuing to implement the terms of the Agreement.

The reaction of unionists was more deeply felt and sustained. Unionists were almost unanimously opposed to the formal involvement by the Republic in the administration of Northern Ireland and felt betrayed by the apparently total exclusion of their political leaders from the negotiation of the Agreement. Huge numbers, estimated at between 100,000 and 200,000, turned out for a rally in Belfast shortly after the Agreement at which the Rev. Ian Paisley declared that unionists would 'never, never, never' accept the Agreement. Soon after loyalists paramilitary groups and others mounted a 'day of action' during which roadblocks and other demonstrations brought commercial life in many parts of Northern Ireland to a standstill. There were fears at the time that a campaign of intimidation against members of the RUC, and the personal opposition to the Agreement which many policemen undoubtedly felt, might lead to difficulties in law enforcement. But these proved unfounded and the level of public disorder and terrorism directly associated with the Agreement gradually declined.

Opposition to the Agreement at a political level was maintained over a much longer period. Under the general slogan of 'Ulster Says No' all the main unionist parties embarked on a campaign of non-cooperation with British ministers and officials. This led in 1986 to the suspension of the Northern

Ireland Assembly, which had been reconstituted in 1982 under the policy of 'rolling devolution' pursued by the then Secretary of State, James Prior, but had been boycotted by the SDLP and had become little more than a forum for unionist opposition to the Agreement. There were also difficulties in some unionist-controlled district councils which refused to fix rates and to carry out certain other statutory functions. But the structures for intergovernmental consultation under the Agreement were designed to be operable regardless of the extent of non-cooperation or boycott by politicians in Northern Ireland, and after a few years the unionist ban on all dealings with British and Irish ministers and officials was effectively abandoned.

This did not mean that the Agreement could be said to have fulfilled the underlying objective, as set out in the Preamble, of 'diminishing the divisions [in Northern Ireland] and achieving lasting peace and stability'. The level of paramilitary violence on both sides continued much as before and there was now a substantial degree of alienation among unionists as well as nationalists from the processes of government 'by diktat' in Northern Ireland. In their official review of the Agreement in 1989, the two governments re-emphasized their commitment to all aspects of the Agreement. But they also tacitly recognized that intergovernmental cooperation between ministers and officials was not in itself helping to create structures for government in which politicians on both sides would share power and responsibility. Accordingly, they committed themselves to renewed efforts to secure the cooperation of constitutional representatives of both traditions in the devolution of responsibility for certain matters to elected representatives in Northern Ireland and indicated that 'if the objectives of the Agreement could be more effectively served by changes in the scope and nature of the working of the Conference' the two governments would be willing to consider them. This was, in effect, a coded message to unionists that new arrangements could be made to

supersede the Ministerial Conference and Secretariat if unionists were ready to cooperate with them.

The talks process

There followed a lengthy period of 'talks about talks' in which
Peter Brooke, the new Secretary of State, sought to find a
formula for talks which was acceptable both to the two unionist
parties and to the SDLP. Agreement was eventually reached in
1991 on a three-strand 'talks process' in which each of the
three significant relationships would be discussed: talks between the constitutional parties in Northern Ireland to be held
in Belfast and chaired by the British Secretary of State (Strand
1); talks between the Northern Ireland parties and the two
governments to be held in Belfast and Dublin and chaired by an
independent Australian diplomat, Sir Ninian Stevens (Strand
2); and talks between the two governments (Strand 3). It was
also agreed that the talks would be confidential, that 'nothing
would be agreed until everything was agreed', and that while
the talks were under way meetings of the Ministerial Conference were to be suspended for a limited period.

The Strand 1 talks finally got under way in May 1991. All
the Northern Ireland parties made formal presentations. But
little real progress was made before the next meeting of the
Ministerial Conference, which had already been arranged for
July and which neither the Irish government nor the SDLP
were prepared to postpone, led to a lengthy suspension. It was
not until after the British general election in April 1992 that the
talks were resumed. In this round the parties presented more
detailed and theoretically confidential papers on various aspects
of the problem, though most were soon leaked to the press.
The most controversial was the SDLP proposal that Northern
Ireland should be governed by six commissioners, three elected
in Northern Ireland and three appointed respectively by the

British and Irish governments and the European Commission. In the initial stages the proposals of the unionist parties concentrated on more conventional forms of devolution and power-sharing within Northern Ireland and on the need for the Republic of Ireland to abandon its constitutional claim to jurisdiction over Northern Ireland. When it was decided that these Strand 1 talks had made sufficient progress – or rather that they could make no more progress – the talks moved on to Strand 2 and two meetings were held between a ministerial team from the coalition government in Dublin, comprising Fianna Fáil and the Progressive Democrats, and representatives of the four Northern Ireland parties. The first of these was in London and the second in Belfast. The Democratic Unionists refused to attend a later Dublin meeting while the Irish constitutional claim remained. At the Dublin meeting the Official Unionists made new proposals for some possible shared structures between a Northern Ireland government and the Irish government. But the Fianna Fáil ministers were not prepared to make any corresponding concessions and, with an Irish general election in the offing, the talks were again brought to an inconclusive end in November 1992. Though the independent chairman, Sir Ninian Stevens, was able to secure general agreement to a statement that substantial progress had been made on some issues and that the talks could profitably be resumed, the general public perception was that they had failed to achieve any substantial compromise on any of the fundamental issues.

Following the formation of a new coalition government – of Fianna Fáil and the Irish Labour Party – in the Republic in January 1993, there have been repeated attempts to restart the talks process. None had proved successful by the end of 1993. The extent of the difficulty facing the British and Irish governments in this respect is highlighted by the lack of consensus over the reasons for the failure of the talks in 1991 and 1992. The unionist parties have been widely criticized for their uncompromising attitude on the Irish constitutional claim and on the need to remove any 'say' for the Irish government over the internal administration of Northern Ireland as provided under the Anglo-Irish Agreement. The SDLP has likewise been criticized for having stuck rigidly to its initial proposals for the involvement of British, Irish and European commissioners in the internal government of Northern Ireland, and for having in this way 'moved the goalposts' from the objective of internal power-sharing to some form of joint authority. The Irish government has been criticized, not least by opposition parties in Dublin, for its failure to move on the constitutional claim or to respond positively to the final Official Unionist proposals for shared North–South institutions. And the British government has been criticized on all sides for its failure to set out with any clarity the type of settlement which it favours and would be prepared to implement.

Initiative '92 and the Opsahl Commission

There is strong evidence from opinion polls that a large majority of people in Northern Ireland want their politicians to engage in serious talks and to come to an agreement. The widespread feeling of despair at the inability of the party leaders in Northern Ireland to reach a reasonable compromise, and the failure of the British and Irish governments to get them to do so, had already led to the development of a major unofficial peace initiative in 1991. Initiative '92, as it became known, was designed to allow ordinary people, rather than established politicians, to have an effective say in the search for peace. With the support of some major charities in Britain the organizers, Robin Wilson and Simon Lee, were able to establish an independent commission of experts from both parts of Ireland, Britain and the United States under the chairmanship of a leading Norwegian human rights lawyer, Professor Torkel

Opsahl. With the slogan 'No one ever asked you till now', interested individuals and groups were invited to make written submissions to the Opsahl Commission during 1992. A good indication of the interest in the initiative was the fact that more than 500 submissions were made, rather more than the number achieved by the official New Ireland Forum in 1983. This was followed by a series of public hearings early in 1993 at which those who had made major submissions were questioned on them by the commissioners.

The Opsahl Commission Report was published in June 1993.[15] One part of the report was a comprehensive summary of the submissions and hearings which made it clear, if there had been any doubt, that there is no more general consensus on what should be done to achieve peace and stability among the individuals and groups who participated in the Opsahl process than among the politicians. The commissioners themselves, however, were able to agree on some general conclusions in the light of what they had heard from both major communities and those between. One of the most significant was that, since the unionist community was not going to accept an executive role for the Irish government within Northern Ireland, its government should be based on the principle that each community should have an equal voice in making and executing laws or a veto on their execution, and an equal share in administrative authority. Acceptance of this by the nationalist community, however, would require legal recognition of the legitimacy of nationalism and formal provision for parity of esteem between the two communities. The commissioners also recommended that ways should be found to involve representatives of Sinn Féin in any future talks, provided they renounced the use of violence. They added that, if the current talks process failed, the British government in consultation with the Irish government should establish an official commission to prepare proposals which would form the basis of further discussions with the major parties and, if necessary, of direct consultation with the people of Northern Ireland. The commissioners' acceptance of the equal rights of both communities also led them to suggest that any future settlement would have to be approved by a majority in both communities, rather than merely by a majority of the people of Northern Ireland. This same principle of equality also lay behind a number of other recommendations, notably on the need for the creation of structures for policing which would involve both communities and for greater emphasis on integration and sharing in education.

The Opsahl Report, as was perhaps predictable, was given a lukewarm reception by the main political parties, not least due to a somewhat insensitive recommendation on the need for better training for politicians. But three coordinated opinion polls carried out in Northern Ireland, the Republic of Ireland and Britain indicated that the reaction of ordinary people to the Opsahl proposals would be more favourable.[16] There was a high level of support for the principle of equality in government from both communities in Northern Ireland (86 per cent of Catholics and 46 per cent of Protestants) and in Britain (67 per cent) and the Irish Republic (81 per cent). There were similarly positive responses to most of the other major proposals. This in itself provides further support for the Opsahl Commission's view that it may be both necessary and desirable to test general public reaction to proposals for the future government of Northern Ireland rather than relying exclusively on talks with political leaders.

The Hume–Adams proposals

There have been many attempts since 1969 to deal directly with the paramilitary leaders on both sides in an attempt to persuade them to give up their campaigns of violence. The British government talked directly to IRA leaders, specially

released from prison for the purpose, in 1972. Groups of
Protestant clergymen have held more or less formal talks with
IRA leaders, notably at Feakle in 1974. Others committed to
the peaceful resolution of conflicts of all kinds, like the Quak-
ers, have maintained contacts and arranged unpublicized meetings with paramilitaries and their political representatives on
both sides. None of these initiatives, however, has had much
observable or lasting impact on the continuation of the conflict,
perhaps because those involved were not in a position to enter
into real political negotiation of the kind which paramilitary
leaders might be interested in.

The more recent series of discussions between John Hume
of the SDLP and Gerry Adams of Sinn Féin are more significant
precisely because they involve political leaders with the capacity
to make and perhaps to deliver a deal in exchange for the
calling-off of violence. The Hume–Adams talks were initiated
in April 1988 with a series of meetings at which papers were
exchanged between the SDLP and Sinn Féin on their respective
approaches to the use of violence, to the British presence in
Northern Ireland and to the fact that about one million of the
five million people in Ireland were implacably opposed to Irish
unification. This round of talks was broken off six months
later without any apparent progress having been made towards
agreement on any of the main issues, though both sides claimed
to have reached some measure of mutual understanding.

The discussions were resumed early in 1993 on a more
individual basis between John Hume and Gerry Adams. In
April, a joint communiqué was issued in which both men
signified their agreement on a number of points: that the
British government no longer had any strategic interest in
maintaining its presence in Northern Ireland; that the Irish
people had the right to determine their own future; and that
peace could only come about if the respective interests and
identities of the unionist and national communities in Northern
Ireland were respected. The reference in this joint statement to

the traditional republican claim of the right of the Irish people to self-determination, though the way in which it might be exercised was not spelled out, caused a storm of protest from unionists and contributed substantially to their fear that a 'pan-nationalist front' was being developed. The talks then appear to have continued at a less intense level until they were abruptly suspended in September, so that a report might be made to the Irish government and through it to the British government. This report was made in mid-October, after a pre-planned visit by John Hume to the United States during which he sought American support for the initiative. It has subsequently emerged that the Irish government was indirectly involved in the formulation of what has become known as the Hume–Adams document.

Though the details of the Hume–Adams proposals have yet to be released, it appears that they involved an understanding that Sinn Féin would use its best efforts to call an end to the IRA campaign in return for the reiteration by the British government that they have no interest in maintaining any presence in Ireland, an acceptance of the legitimacy and value of a united Ireland, a commitment to the principle of self-determination for the people of Ireland to be exercised with the consent of those in both parts of Ireland, and an undertaking that they would implement any agreement reached between representatives of unionists and nationalists on future constitutional structures for both parts of Ireland. At the time of writing, however, it was not clear whether the Hume–Adams proposals also involved the acceptance of some form of joint authority by the British and Irish governments over Northern Ireland or agreement on British withdrawal within a specified time or as a long-term objective.

British talks with Sinn Féin and the IRA

The British government was careful to distance itself from the Hume–Adams proposals and, throughout the summer and autumn of 1993, repeatedly stressed its refusal to have anything to do with negotiations with Sinn Féin or the IRA until they had renounced the use of violence. In November 1993, however, it came to light that the British government had not only maintained a confidential channel of communication with the IRA for many years but also that it had been involved in an extended exchange of communications with leading figures in Sinn Féin and the IRA throughout 1993. As on previous occasions when a direct dialogue with the IRA had been organized, notably before and during the IRA cease-fire in 1972 and throughout the hunger strike period in 1981, a number of different contacts were used involving both members of the secret service and senior civil servants. The government claimed that the dialogue had been initiated in February 1993 by a message from the IRA that it was ready to discuss methods of ending the conflict. Though the precise content of this and other messages is a matter of dispute, it seems clear from the documents which have been published and acknowledged on both sides that both the IRA and the British government were setting out and exploring their respective positions rather than engaging in direct negotiations on the terms for a ceasefire or cessation of violence. This process too, like the Hume–Adams proposals, has been effectively subsumed in the discussion leading to the Downing Street Declaration.

The Downing Street Declaration

The Joint Declaration made by John Major and Albert Reynolds on 15 December 1993 was a direct response to the Hume–Adams initiative. Much of the declaration is designed to encourage the IRA to abandon its armed campaign, and thus to allow Sinn Féin to join the normal political process, by the use of words and concepts which form part of the republican movement's analysis of partition and its justification for the use of violence. That analysis is based on the idea that the partition of Ireland was imposed by the British government in pursuit of its strategic and imperialist interests and was a denial of the right of the Irish people to self-determination. The main focus of the Declaration is thus on the issue of self-determination and the nature of British involvement in Northern Ireland.

The key passages of the Declaration are those in which the two governments have sought to bring together the republican conception of the nature of the right of self-determination with that to which both governments committed themselves in the Anglo-Irish Agreement. This has resulted in a formulation which stresses that decisions on constitutional structures must be placed in the hands of the people of Ireland (reflecting the republican conception of self-determination) but must be exercised with the consent of the people of Northern Ireland (reflecting the governmental commitments in the Anglo-Irish Agreement). Though the parallel statements by the British and Irish governments express this in slightly different ways, their essential effect is identical:

The British government agree that it is for the people of the island of Ireland alone, by agreement between the two parts respectively, to exercise their right of self-determination on the basis of consent, freely and concurrently given, North and South, to bring about a united Ireland, if that is their wish.
(Para. 4)

He [the Taoiseach] accepts on behalf of the Irish government that the democratic right of self-determination by the people of Ireland as a whole must be achieved and exercised with and subject to the agreement and consent of a majority of the people of Northern Ireland.
(Para. 5)

The response to the second key republican concern lies in the British government's statements that they 'have no selfish, strategic or economic interest in Northern Ireland', that 'their primary interest is to see peace, stability and reconciliation established by agreement among all the people who inhabit the island', that 'they will encourage, facilitate and enable the achievement of such agreement', which may 'as of right take the form of agreed structures for the island as a whole, including a united Ireland achieved by peaceful means', and that they will as a binding obligation introduce the legislation necessary to give effect to this or to any other measure of agreement on future relationships in Ireland. These statements make it clear that the British government has not accepted that there can be any pre-determined outcome, notably that of Irish unification, to the process of self-determination. This open-ended approach is less explicit in the statement by the Irish government accepting that 'it would be wrong to attempt to impose a united Ireland in the absence of the freely given consent of a majority of the people of Northern Ireland'. But there is nothing in the Declaration which commits the Irish government to that or any other outcome.

The remainder of the Declaration is concerned with more general statements similar to those in the Anglo-Irish Agreement in which both governments recognize the fears of both major communities in Northern Ireland and commit themselves to work together to heal past divisions and to create conditions in which reconciliation between the nationalist and unionist traditions is possible. But there are few pointers as to precisely how this is to be achieved. The Irish government's undertaking to support changes in 'those elements in the Irish Constitution which are deeply resented by unionists' – notably Articles 2 and 3 – is made conditional on an overall settlement which includes a 'balanced constitutional accommodation'. Nor is it made clear whether the list of essential civil rights and liberties for both communities referred to by the Irish government, including the right to seek constitutional change by peaceful and legitimate means, is intended to be seen in the context of a unified Ireland or of Northern Ireland within the United Kingdom. And there is little detail on the precise role of the Forum for Peace and Reconciliation which the Irish government undertakes to establish, presumably in reaction to the reference in the Hume—Adams proposals to the establishment of an all-Ireland conference to seek agreement on new political structures. The relationship of the proposed Forum to the continuing three-strand talks process which is also referred to in the Declaration is uncertain.

The conciliatory language in the Declaration and its emphasis on people rather than territory has been generally well received by politicians and ordinary people not only in Britain and the Republic of Ireland but also in Northern Ireland. An opinion poll in the Republic indicated that 97 per cent of those asked supported the Declaration. In Northern Ireland the substance of the Declaration, though not all of its wording, has been welcomed by the Ulster Unionist Party and many ordinary unionists. The major objections have been raised by the Rev. Ian Paisley and the Democratic Unionists. At the time of writing the most important reaction, from Sinn Féin and the IRA, had yet to be given. The IRA made a point of continuing its attacks on the security forces and on commercial property. Sinn Féin made a point of the need to have wide consultations throughout the republican movement and to obtain clarification of some aspects of the Declaration, not least the crucial issue of how self-determination is to be exercised.

CHAPTER 5

The European Context

Northern Ireland may be a place apart, but it is not isolated
from the wider world. It is subject to many of the same
economic, social and political pressures as other parts of Ireland, Britain and Europe. As a region within the European
Union many of its economic and social policies are determined
in Brussels rather than in Belfast, Dublin or London. It faces
many of the same problems in protecting individual and communal rights as arise in other ethnic frontier zones. Whatever its
constitutional status within the United Kingdom or a united
Ireland, it will be subject to and a beneficiary of European
standards on democracy, human rights and minority protection
developed within the Council of Europe and the Conference
for Security and Cooperation in Europe. All of these issues –
Northern Ireland's economic position, its place within the
European Union and the growing impact of international standards on democracy, human rights and the treatment of minorities – are as important for many practical purposes as the three
interlocking dimensions – the internal dimension, the North–
South dimension and the British–Irish dimension – identified
as the basis for the current talks process. The Downing Street
Declaration specifically acknowledges that 'the development of
Europe will, of itself, require new approaches to serve interests
common to both parts of the island of Ireland, and to Ireland
and the United Kingdom as partners in the European Union'.
No realistic proposals for a settlement can ignore this wider
international economic and political framework.

The main question on the economic front is whether the

natural forces for economic integration are likely to assist the search for political compromise. For large national and multinational businesses Northern Ireland is a tiny market-place. But it is also a potential location for production given its relatively low labour costs and attractive incentives. The continuing 'troubles' are clearly a factor in business decisions on new capital investment. But they do not affect the day-to-day operations of most established businesses which are increasingly conducted with little regard either for national frontiers or for arguments over national identity. What relevance have these pressures from the business community for a potential political settlement?

The impact of the European Union is closely linked to these economic influences. Many of the major decisions that affect the viability of particular enterprises, not least in the agricultural sector, are made at a European level in complex deals struck by the representatives of the member states. But the European Commission is committed to a policy of increasing the recognition and representation of distinctive regions within member states and also to diminishing the adverse influence of frontiers between states. What relevance have these policies for the future status of a place like Northern Ireland which falls between two states?

The final issue in this context is the potential impact of the growing body of international standards on democracy, individual human rights and the treatment of distinctive peoples and minorities. The principles of democracy and self-determination are powerful factors in any conflict over how people in a given territory should be governed even if there is no consensus on how they should be applied. Events in what was Yugoslavia, in the Czech and Slovak Republics and elsewhere, have reminded us that separation into smaller units on ethnic or other grounds cannot be ruled out as a means of resolving communal conflict despite the external economic and political forces for integration. There is also a growing body of international principles and conventions on the rights of individuals and the treatment of minorities. Both the British and Irish governments are parties to most of the relevant international instruments and organizations in this sphere. What is the relevance of these aspects of international law and policy to the potential for a settlement in Northern Ireland based either on greater separation or on greater sharing?

Economic dimensions

It is sometimes argued that the Northern Ireland economy is in terminal decline. That is an oversimplification. Its position is worse than that of other depressed regions within the United Kingdom, but not a great deal worse. It is economically better off than many other regions in Europe, including Ireland, not least due to the substantial internal transfers within the United Kingdom, which are proportionally very much greater than those within the European Union.

Northern Ireland has not always been economically depressed. At the turn of the twentieth century Belfast and the surrounding area was one of the more prosperous industrial areas in Great Britain or Ireland. The industrialization of linen and other textile production began later in Northern Ireland than in other areas in Britain. There was also a thriving shipbuilding and engineering industry. The 'black North', as it was known, was far ahead of any other part of Ireland in commercial and industrial development. Housing and other social conditions in Belfast compared favourably with those in other large industrial centres in England and Scotland. Farming standards were also generally better and farms were larger than in the rest of Ireland, due to the long-established Ulster tenant rights which had encouraged improvements and the consolidation of holdings by tenants long before Gladstone's land reforms of the 1870s.

The decline from this relatively favourable position – under which the Protestant community generally fared much better than the Catholic community – began in the 1930s and continued rapidly with the sharp decline in the linen and shipbuilding industries in the 1950s and 1960s. By that time Northern Ireland was already an unemployment blackspot in the United Kingdom. The Northern Ireland government sought to remedy the decline by offering incentives to large multinational companies to locate their man-made fibre production in Northern Ireland. This policy was relatively successful. But these factories were often the first to be closed down in times of recession. The onset of the troubles in the 1970s made it all the more difficult to attract inward investment to replace jobs in these declining industries. It has been estimated that the 'troubles' and the resulting loss of international confidence in Northern Ireland as a location for production resulted in the 'loss' of 46,000 jobs that might otherwise have existed.[1] The disappointing performance in this respect of the Industrial Development Board (IDB) in Northern Ireland is in stark contrast to the relative success of the Industrial Development Authority (IDA) in the Republic of Ireland in attracting high-technology jobs, though at a high cost to the Irish Exchequer. The result has been that between 1950 and 1990 employment in manufacturing in Northern Ireland declined from almost 200,000 or 36 per cent of total employment to just over 100,000 or 18 per cent of the total.[2] This was not appreciably larger, however, than the comparable figures for Great Britain in the same period which showed a decline in manufacturing employment from 51 per cent to 22 per cent.

In many respects the performance of the Northern Ireland economy in this period has thus mirrored that of other parts of the United Kingdom. One major difference has been the continuing growth in the numbers seeking work as a result of the increase in the population and the decline in emigration. Despite this, however, the employment rate in Northern Ireland has maintained a remarkably stable relationship with that in Great Britain, at around 5 percentage points higher than the overall United Kingdom average. For example, in the 1970s the unemployment rate in Northern Ireland varied between 4 per cent and 10 per cent compared with figures of 2 per cent and 6 per cent for Great Britain; the comparable figures for the 1980s were between 12 per cent and 18 per cent for Northern Ireland and 6 per cent and 12 per cent for the UK. The explanation for this relative stability lies in the very rapid growth in public sector employment. It has been estimated that in 1960 just short of 100,000 people, or 22 per cent of the total in employment, in Northern Ireland were employed by the public sector; by 1991 this had increased to some 175,000, or 38 per cent of the total.[3] Many of these jobs have been in education, health and related services and have helped to create a prosperous Catholic middle class. But much of the very rapid increase in the public sector since 1970 has been in security-related jobs. It has been estimated, for example, that between 1970 and 1985 some 35,000 public sector jobs were created as a direct or indirect consequence of the 'troubles'.[4] One of the continuing imponderables in this context is whether there would be an 'employment dividend' in manufacturing and other sectors from a political settlement sufficient to offset the decline in security-related employment which would follow if peace broke out.

It would not have been possible for this decline in employment in manufacturing to have been offset to this extent by increases in public sector employment if Northern Ireland had not, as part of the United Kingdom, received substantial transfers of funds from the British Exchequer. It is difficult to be precise about the total amount of these transfers. Most taxes are collected on a United Kingdom basis and Northern Ireland is clearly entitled to a share in the public sector spending which those taxes make possible. But there is no doubt that Northern Ireland receives in its public spending allocation much more than its taxpayers contribute. In the papers for the

Northern Ireland Convention in 1974 the subvention was stated to have risen from £52 million in 1966–7 to £313 million in 1973–4. This represented just over one-third (37 per cent) of total public sector expenditure in Northern Ireland in 1973–4. By 1983, according to figures prepared for the New Ireland Forum, the subvention had risen to some £1,420 million, including extra Army expenditure of £140 million, representing a similar proportion (37 per cent) of total public expenditure. By 1992–3 the official estimate of the subvention had risen to some £3,500 million, including some £300 million additional Army costs, representing almost half (47 per cent) of total public expenditure of £7,500 million.[5] Throughout the period, however, the assessment of the true extent of the subvention has been complicated by the fact that almost all expenditure by Northern Ireland departments including capital items are met directly by the annual allocation from the British Exchequer, with the result that borrowing and interest payments remain comparatively low. For example, some £1,500 million of the subvention for 1992–3 can be said to represent Northern Ireland's share of the total UK budget deficit of some £50 billion. If Northern Ireland were a separate self-financing unit on a par with the Republic of Ireland or part of a united Ireland, a higher proportion of its expenditure would probably be covered by borrowing. It should also be noted, as will be seen below, that these internal transfers within the United Kingdom are much greater than current European transfers to the UK under the European Regional Development and Social Funds in respect of Northern Ireland which from 1989 to 1993 have totalled about £130 million per year.

The resulting level of prosperity in Northern Ireland at the end of the 1980s can best be assessed by comparing it with some other regions both in the United Kingdom and in other European Union states. The usual measure for this purpose is gross domestic product per head, or the average income of those resident in the area. On this basis the figure for Northern

Ireland in 1990 was 74 per cent of the European Community average, compared with figures of 84 per cent for Wales, 87 per cent for the north of England, 93 per cent for Scotland, and 121 per cent for the southeast of England. The comparable figure for the Republic of Ireland was 68 per cent. But there were many other regions in the European Community with comparable or lower figures than Northern Ireland: the Oost-Nederland region in the Netherlands (85 per cent), the Wallonie region in Belgium (85 per cent), the five southern regions in Italy (Campania 69 per cent; Abruzzi/Molise 87 per cent; Sud 69 per cent; Sicilia 66 per cent and Sardegna 74 per cent), and the whole of Spain (75 per cent), Portugal (56 per cent) and Greece (47 per cent).[6] Northern Ireland may be the least prosperous region in the United Kingdom, but its position in the United Kingdom results in internal transfers of resources which make it relatively well off compared with many other European regions.

The dependence of Northern Ireland on the United Kingdom economy can also be seen by looking at patterns of trade. Most of Northern Ireland's imports and exports for many years came from or went to other parts of the United Kingdom. Until recently there was relatively little cross-border trade with the Republic or direct trade with other European countries. With the development of the single European market, however, this picture is changing rapidly. There is now an increasing flow of goods and of capital across the border. Estimated figures for 1990 are that of some £6,000 million worth of goods manufactured in Northern Ireland some £4,000 million were exported; but of these some £2,000 million went to Great Britain and only about £400 million to the Republic; almost double that amount, some £750 million, was exported from the Republic to Northern Ireland.[7] There have been a number of substantial business take-overs and amalgamations designed to create all-Ireland marketing and distribution units, notably in the dairy and supermarket sectors. Considerable efforts are being made by the business community both to promote and develop these cross-border trading and organizational links and also to make it clear that they are entirely independent and without any political or constitutional implications. But these cross-border links are still very much less significant than those which link the Northern Irish economy with that of the rest of the United Kingdom. Most large enterprises operating in Northern Ireland are subsidiaries or divisions of British companies and the business cycle in Northern Ireland is dominated by trends in the British economy as a whole. But this may not always be the case. Larger companies in many sectors are increasingly managing their production, marketing and distribution on an all-Ireland basis.

The most obvious conclusion from this brief economic survey is that Northern Ireland has long been and currently remains closely integrated with and dependent on the overall British economy, both in its public sector finances and in more general commercial and industrial terms. The most obvious benefit to Northern Ireland from this is the continuing high level of subvention from the British taxpayer. But there are some countervailing costs, notably the difficulties faced by policy makers in developing and pursuing their own economic strategies, for example, in respect of agriculture, and the fact that plants in Northern Ireland are often the first to be closed in a recession. In these and other respects the Northern Ireland economy is more like that of the Republic of Ireland, which also has a substantial agricultural sector and a pressing need to attract foreign investment to maintain employment. On issues of this kind there is likely to be an advantage in a closer economic alliance or integration with the Republic. In economic as in many other matters Northern Ireland falls somewhere between the rest of the United Kingdom and the rest of Ireland so that its best interests may better be served by recognizing and accommodating both these differing perspectives.

The European Union

There has been considerable interest in recent years in the idea that the problems of divergent allegiances and aspirations in Northern Ireland might in some way be alleviated or resolved within the wider European Union. The European Community was initially established with a view to resolving the historic conflict between France and Germany by building new economic and political links between them without prescribing any specific end result. A similar approach may be appropriate in respect of the historic conflict between Britain and Ireland. At the simplest level it may be argued that the conflict between the British and Irish identities of the two communities might become irrelevant as people see themselves primarily as Europeans rather than as British or Irish citizens. It has also been argued that the British subvention might gradually be replaced by European subventions. The idea of some form of distinctive regional status for Northern Ireland, which might be developed within a 'Europe of the Regions', has also been relied on as a means of resolving the conflicting constitutional claims of the British and Irish states over the territory of Northern Ireland. The most dramatic formulation of this was the proposal formally tabled by the SDLP during the talks in 1992 that the European Community might become directly involved in the government of Northern Ireland through the appointment of a commissioner to share authority with a British minister, an Irish minister and three elected Northern Ireland politicians.

How realistic are these various suggestions? Can the European Union play an active role in the search for a settlement in Northern Ireland, or is it limited to providing relatively minor economic assistance and general political support to the British and Irish governments in their search for a political deal? And has the wrangle over the Maastricht Treaty of Union and the unresolved issue of the proposed single European currency any relevance to Northern Ireland?

The fact that both the United Kingdom and the Republic of Ireland joined the European Union in 1973 has already had a positive impact on their relationship over Northern Ireland. The regular contacts between British and Irish ministers on an equal footing in meetings of the Council of Ministers has helped to reduce the previously unbalanced and historically soured relationship between them. The commitment within the Community to the peaceful resolution of historical enmities like those between France and Germany provided a useful example and some welcome pressure towards cooperation and compromise rather than confrontation. Similarly, at a more practical level the encouragement of cross-border economic development has fostered better relationships at a local level in border counties. This new cooperative relationship was cemented in the Anglo-Irish Agreement of 1985, which referred explicitly in its Preamble to the joint wish of the two states 'to develop the unique relationship between their peoples and the close cooperation between their countries as friendly neighbours and as partners in the European Community'. The fact that the United Kingdom and the Republic of Ireland have given up some of their sovereignty both on their accession to the original Treaty of Rome in 1973 and under the Single European Act in 1987 may also assist by showing that absolutist notions of state sovereignty are no longer as essential to national survival as they were once thought to be.

The European Union is also committed to helping to reduce economic inequality between its member states. A major contribution in this respect has been made by the common agricultural policy under which farmers on both sides of the border in Ireland have prospered. But substantial grants have also been paid under the European Regional Development and Social Funds for projects on both sides of the border. The sums involved, however, have been relatively small, amounting from 1989 to 1993 in the case of Northern Ireland to some £130 million per year and in the case of the Republic to some £660 million per year. This is despite the fact that Northern Ireland has been granted relatively favourable status as an 'Objective 1' area for the purposes of the Regional Development Fund to which it is not strictly entitled in terms of its gross national product per head after the receipt of the British subvention. The decision of the Community to grant Objective 1 status to both parts of Ireland was an indication of its willingness to be flexible and to treat Northern Ireland as a special case. But as has already been pointed out, even this favourable European subvention is small compared to the general and continuing subvention to Northern Ireland from the British Exchequer.

The provisions of the Maastricht Treaty of Union will develop these ideological and practical incentives for cooperation over Northern Ireland still further. It increases the range of matters on which member states have agreed to share their sovereignty and decision making. It makes express provision for a new formal status of European citizenship. It introduces further provisions for the recognition and representation of regions within the Union. And it extends and develops the structures for achieving further and more rapid steps towards greater economic equality by providing for a new Cohesion Fund. All this, it should be noted, is quite separate from the provisions in respect of European Monetary Union over which there has been so much continuing dispute and which are now widely regarded as unlikely ever to be implemented in their present form.

The new concept of European citizenship may help in resolving some of the issues arising from the choice between British and Irish citizenship that is open to all individuals born in Northern Ireland under the relevant British and Irish nationality legislation. Some nationalists have argued that if Articles 2 and 3 of the Irish Constitution were amended to withdraw any formal claim to jurisdiction over Northern Ireland, the right of those in Northern Ireland to assert their Irish citizenship might be affected. Most of the practical problems which may arise over citizenship will be covered by the provisions of the Maastricht Treaty. These provide that every person holding the citizenship of a member state shall be a citizen of the European Union (Article 8) and as such shall have the right to move and reside freely within the territory of all member states (Article 8a), to vote and stand as a candidate at local elections in any state in which he or she is residing under the same conditions as nationals of that state (Article 8b), to receive diplomatic protection abroad from the officials of any member state (Article 8c) and to petition the European Parliament or Ombudsman (Article 8d). Whether these new European citizenship rights will be sufficient to remove the symbolic as opposed to the practical aspects of national citizenship is more doubtful. Many unionists and nationalists in Northern Ireland will certainly wish to continue to assert their British and Irish identities and it will probably be necessary to make specific provision to preserve the existing dual-citizenship rights in any new British–Irish Agreement which removed or amended Articles 2 and 3 of the Irish Constitution.

Europe of the Regions

The Maastricht Treaty also makes formal provision for the recognition and representation of regions as distinctive entities within the European Union by establishing a Committee of the Regions.[8] The purpose of this body is to continue and extend the work of the previously established Consultative Council of Regional and Local Authorities. The new Committee is to have 189 members nominated by member states, of which 24 will be from the United Kingdom and nine from the Republic of Ireland. It has recently been agreed that two of the twenty-four United Kingdom nominations will be from Northern Ireland.

But the final power to make nominations will remain with the member states and there is no obligation on them to create or recognize territorial regions for that purpose. The Republic, for example, has always been treated as a single region for European Union purposes and it does not appear that this will be altered under the new regional structures. Furthermore, the functions of the Committee will be exclusively consultative and advisory. The power of decision making and the allocation of Union resources and grants will remain the responsibility of member states.

Considerable development of the concept of regions as independent entities for financial or other purposes would be necessary before any special status for Northern Ireland within a 'Europe of the Regions' could be envisaged. This does not, of course, exclude the possibility that some special provision might be made for the separate recognition or representation of Northern Ireland if it were proposed by the United Kingdom and the Republic and agreed to by other member states. But the initiative for this would almost certainly have to come from the two governments and there might be considerable resistance from other member states fearful of creating a precedent for other potentially independent regions or disputed territories.

The most important part of the Maastricht Treaty from an Irish point of view is probably the proposed new Structural and Cohesion Funds. The Irish government hopes to receive payments amounting to some IR£8 billion over a six-year period under this new regime, an expectation which played a large part in the eventual Yes vote in the Irish referendum on Maastricht. Northern Ireland, as part of the United Kingdom, however, is in a much less favourable position in this respect, since only those countries whose gross domestic product is less than 90 per cent of the Community average can qualify for this level of payment. Northern Ireland's share of the same funds over the same period is expected to amount to some £1.2

billion. But if Northern Ireland were to be treated as a special regional unit or if it were to become part of a united Ireland, it would not be unreasonable to expect that larger levels of European support would be forthcoming on a par with that for the Republic.

A further possibility, discussed below, is that the European Union might act as a guarantor of a settlement between the British and Irish governments, and thus reassure both unionists and nationalists in Northern Ireland that a new British–Irish Agreement supplementing or replacing the Anglo-Irish Agreement of 1985 and setting out the respective rights of members of the two communities would not be abandoned by future British and Irish governments without the consent of those affected. But this falls outside the current competence of the Union and might meet some resistance from other member states even if the British and Irish governments proposed it.

All these possibilities will be discussed further below. For the present it is sufficient to conclude that the European Union is unlikely in the immediate future to become an active participant in the creation of new constitutional structures for a place like Northern Ireland. It may be better to think of it as a framework within which the almost exclusive financial dependence of Northern Ireland on the British Exchequer may gradually be diminished, and more generally as a model for interstate cooperation on an open-ended basis without any very clear constitutional objective in view.

International standards

Northern Ireland's place in Europe means that other significant international standards and pressures must be taken into account in any new settlement. Both the United Kingdom and the Republic of Ireland are members of the Council of Europe and participants in the Conference on Security and Cooperation in Europe (CSCE). Both these bodies impose obligations on their members, not only in respect of basic individual human rights, but also increasingly on collective and communal rights in respect of democratic institutions and the treatment of minorities. These international standards clearly impose some constraints on those involved in drawing up the details of any proposed settlement for Northern Ireland. But they may also afford significant opportunities for international assistance in guaranteeing and monitoring the implementation of any settlement.

The Council of Europe

The Council of Europe was established in 1949 with a full range of institutions – a Council of Ministers, a Parliamentary Assembly and a Human Rights Court – in the hope that it might develop into a powerful all-purpose European body. That potential was soon overtaken by the separate development of the much smaller and more economically oriented European Economic Community, the forerunner of what is now the European Union. But the Council of Europe has continued to operate and now has thirty-two member states, including the new democracies in Eastern Europe. Its major role lies in the promotion of political and legal cooperation through a wide range of international conventions open to all member states in Europe.

The most important of these is the European Convention on Human Rights and Fundamental Freedoms which has established the principle, hitherto unknown in international law, that individual citizens may enforce the rights created under the Convention against their own governments through the European Commission and Court of Human Rights at Strasbourg. This Convention has already had a significant impact on security and other policies adopted by the British government throughout the current conflict in Northern Ireland, as explained in Chapter 3. The rights recognized under the Convention are none the less somewhat limited. They exclude many matters of particular importance in Northern Ireland, notably protection against economic discrimination, protection against certain forms of emergency law, and guarantees on most collective or communal rights.

Some of these limitations are covered under other existing or proposed Council of Europe conventions. The European Convention on the Suppression of Terrorism of 1977 has already had an important impact on arrangements for the extradition of terrorist suspects between the United Kingdom and the Republic of Ireland. The European Convention on the Prevention of Torture of 1989 provides a permanent monitoring procedure by which preventive action may be taken in situations where there is a risk of torture or inhuman or degrading treatment, as, for example, the police interrogation centres at Castlereagh and Armagh.[9] The European Charter on Regional and Minority Languages of 1992 is clearly of relevance to the status of the Irish language in Northern Ireland. And at the Vienna summit of the Council of Europe Heads of State in September 1993 it was agreed that a new convention on the protection of the cultural rights of minorities in Europe should be prepared.

An equally important potential role for the Council of Europe may be in helping to guarantee and adjudicate on individual and communal rights aspects of any new British–Irish agreement on Northern Ireland. It might be possible, for instance, for the Council of Europe to incorporate relevant aspects of such a settlement in a Protocol to the European Convention on Human Rights, thus making it possible for disputes to be dealt with by the existing procedures before the Commission or Court at Strasbourg. Alternatively, it might be possible for a special commission or court to be set up with representatives from Strasbourg, as was proposed and in principle agreed in the Vance–Owen plan for Bosnia. Some form of recognition by the Council of Europe of the individual and communal rights aspects of a settlement in Northern Ireland and the possibility of referring disputes to an independent external adjudicatory body distinct from the British and Irish courts might assist in giving confidence to both communities that the terms of a settlement could not be ignored or over-ridden by future British or Irish governments.

The Conference on Security and Cooperation in Europe (CSCE)

The CSCE is the least well known of the new European institutions of relevance to a settlement in Northern Ireland. It originated in the Helsinki Conference of 1973–5 which was intended primarily as a means of increasing cooperation and diminishing the risks of war between the two major power blocs, the Western and the Soviet alliances. It now embraces all the states of Europe, currently fifty-two in number. Both the United Kingdom and the Republic of Ireland have been partici-pants from the start. The Helsinki Final Act of 1975 contained important provisions on individual and democratic rights which played a significant role in the development of democratic regimes in many East European countries in the 1980s. More recently successive CSCE Documents, notably those of Vienna in 1989, Copenhagen in 1990 and Moscow in 1991, have developed more detailed formulations of principles and stand-ards for the promotion of democratic government, the protec-tion of minorities and the avoidance of armed conflict. Those of most direct relevance to Northern Ireland are the provisions of the Copenhagen Document on many aspects of democratic government in general and electoral systems in particular, and on the treatment of minorities.

Unlike the rights protected under the Council of Europe structures, however, these CSCE principles and standards are not legally enforceable in either international or national law and there is no provision for independent adjudication of any kind. The CSCE process depends primarily on diplomatic intervention by member states rather than formal legal action by individuals against their governments. This is based on a new and equally significant limitation on the hitherto sacrosanct principle of state sovereignty, that member states may legitimately concern themselves with and formally question the performance of other states in implementing their commitments under successive CSCE Documents, as set out in the Helsinki Summit Declaration of 1992:

We emphasize that the commitments undertaken under the human rights dimension of the CSCE are matters of direct and legitimate concern to all participating States and do not belong exclusively to the internal affairs of the State concerned.
(Para. 8)

The procedures under which such intervention may be made have been progressively extended. The first step is for a concerned state to raise the issue with the state whose conduct may be in breach of CSCE standards on a bilateral basis. Under the Vienna Document of 1989 the responding state was required to reply to formal requests for information and to hold bilateral meetings on relevant issues. In the Copenhagen Document of 1990 time limits of a maximum of four weeks for responses to formal requests and three weeks for bilateral meetings were set. In the Moscow Document of 1991 these time limits were reduced to ten days and one week respectively, and further provision was made for the appointment of a panel of experts with powers to facilitate the resolution of matters raised, to make visits to the territory of the responding state and to hold confidential discussions with officials, non-governmental organizations and individuals on relevant matters. Under the Helsinki Document of 1992 the task of establishing the panel of experts and facilitating the work of missions was entrusted to the CSCE Office for Democratic Institutions and Human Rights in Warsaw (ODIHR).

The Helsinki Document of 1992 also created the office of a High Commissioner on National Minorities with the task of identifying and helping to resolve potential minority problems before they become a serious threat to peace and security. The Commissioner, Max van der Stoel, has authority to receive reports from organizations representing minorities and to make visits to relevant territories with or without the assistance of expert missions arranged by the Office for Democratic Institutions and Human Rights. But there are two significant limitations: the High Commissioner is not permitted to consider national minority issues 'in situations involving organized acts of terrorism' (Para. 5b) and may not communicate with 'any person or organization which practises or condones terrorism or violence' (Para. 25).

All these principles and mechanisms may be of assistance in monitoring the performance of the authorities and the security forces in Northern Ireland both under the current regime and under any future settlement. Independent external monitoring in respect of allegations of abuses on such matters as harassment, ill-treatment during interrogation and the use of lethal force could assist both in preventing abuses and in increasing public confidence in the security forces. Any difficulty over the limitations on the authority of the High Commissioner on National Minorities in monitoring the effectiveness of any measures to protect the interests of both major communities could be removed with the consent of the British government.

PART III

THE POLICY DILEMMA

Making the basic choice for Northern Ireland between separation of the two communities or sharing by all sections of a single community creates an awkward policy dilemma for the British and Irish governments. Their preferred policy, as set out in the Anglo-Irish Agreement, is to encourage the accommodation and recognition of the two communities, the creation of a devolved government in which representatives of both would share power and responsibility and the development of institutional links between North and South. But the preconditions which the political leaders of both communities have set for their agreement for sharing power within Northern Ireland and for the development of any such links make it difficult to achieve any progress towards that objective. The longer the impasse over the cessation of violence following the Downing Street Declaration and over the political talks process remains, the greater the difficulties created by the slow but cumulative processes of communal separation brought about by the continuing paramilitary activity on both sides.

One response to this might be for the two governments to seek to impose a settlement by moving towards some form of joint authority under which the two governments would share in the administration of Northern Ireland on behalf of the unionist and nationalist communities until their leaders agreed to share in a power-sharing government. This approach was one of the options discussed in the New Ireland Forum Report in 1984 and was proposed in a variant with a European dimension by the SDLP in the talks process in 1992. It has also been mooted by the Labour Party in Britain in a discussion document published in 1993 and elicited a guarded but not wholly dismissive response from Sinn Féin leaders. But it has a number of drawbacks. To impose joint authority would certainly be perceived to constitute a breach of the terms of the Anglo-Irish Agreement which stated that any change in the status of Northern Ireland would only come about with the consent of the people of Northern Ireland. That in itself would be a signal to the unionist community that the guarantees by the two governments of the principle of consent were as worthless as unionist leaders said they were and would make it all the easier for opposition to any proposed arrangements to be mounted on the ground that they were merely a preparation for a total 'sell-out'. It might also lead to further instability and paramilitary activity from loyalists and thus increase the forces of communal separation to a point from which some form of repartition might become more difficult to avoid.

Another response might be to seek to come to some agreement with the paramilitaries or their political fronts with a view to ending the violence and joining in a talks process. This is the thinking which lies behind the talks between John Hume of the SDLP and Gerry Adams for Sinn Féin and the joint governmental peace initiative launched in the Downing Street Declaration. There are good grounds for seeking to persuade all paramilitaries to abandon the use of violence and to negotiate a settlement. But there are also substantial dangers. If the paramilitaries on one side are able to exact a price for their cessation of violence, those on the other may respond by escalating their campaign until they can demand an equivalent concession. The involvement of the 'hard men' in the talks process creates a risk that any resulting settlement would be based on separation rather than sharing, as it has done both in Bosnia and in Palestine.

If neither of these currently prominent policy options is likely to achieve the objective of a settlement based on communal sharing, what are the governments to do? To continue with the current status quo – continuing direct rule from Westminster with continuing uncertainty as to the nature of a longer-term settlement – on an indefinite basis is equally unlikely to stem the slow but steady movement towards increasing communal separation. If a settlement is to be based on sharing rather than separation, it is more likely to be achieved by building on those in the centre rather than those on the extremes. Given the relative weakness of the political parties in the centre that can probably be achieved only by seeking to mobilize the much larger body of opinion which appears to exist in favour of communal sharing. That points to the use of one or more popular referendums as the best way of finding out whether there is sufficient popular support for sharing on which to base a settlement. And if there is not, it may be better to move deliberately as a matter of policy towards greater separation.

In the chapters in this final part the practicalities of these various approaches will be analysed in greater detail, not only in terms of the desirability of the final outcome but also in terms of the way in which it might be brought about. That will demand some new thinking, not only on the structures for government and for intergovernmental relations at all levels but also on the political processes by which they are to be achieved.

CHAPTER 6

Structures for Sharing

There is no difficulty in suggesting structures which could provide for and encourage sharing at all levels of government between communal representatives in a divided society like Northern Ireland. All kinds of formal and informal constitutional mechanisms have been developed and operated with greater or lesser success in other countries. In Belgium, as will be seen, a system of strict proportional allocation of governmental portfolios and powers and complex weighted majority voting requirements has been developed for the sharing of powers on certain essential matters at a national level between French and Dutch speakers; entirely different mechanisms based on communal separation operate at lower levels of government. In Holland, sharing between Protestants and Catholics at national level is based on an informal 'grand compromise' reached in 1917, though local government is operated on the more usual principles of majority rule.

It cannot, of course, be assumed that what works in one country or at one level of government will work in other countries or at other levels. Experience elsewhere can provide useful ideas for alternatives to the simple majority rule systems that have been developed in more homogeneous societies like Britain and the Republic. But no two divided societies are the same. Structures for sharing must reflect the nature of the divisions between the communities and the extent of intermingling between them. The challenge for those who are committed to sharing rather than separation is to find a particular set of structures within which the major parties are prepared to work together at the various levels of government. Constitutional structures for communal cooperation are unlikely to survive for long if the representatives of any major community are determined to make them unworkable. The carefully constructed arrangements for communal power-sharing in Cyprus, for example, collapsed in the face of a refusal by the Turkish Cypriot parties to cooperate in the raising and allocation of finance for government.

Sharing power at the regional level

The major problem in developing structures for sharing power in Northern Ireland has been the difficulty in reaching agreement among the main parties on one of the wide range of potentially workable systems for regional government. Two broad approaches have thus far been pursued by the various parties to the talks process. The first, which is favoured by the main unionist parties, by the Alliance Party and probably by the British government, may be called the internal power-sharing model. The second, which is favoured by the SDLP, by some sections of the British Labour Party and probably by the Irish government, may be called the externally shared authority model. Elements of both can, of course, be combined. And many of the structures for sharing at lower levels of government and public administration – in education, in housing and in employment – will be the same under either. But the advantages and disadvantages of the two models can most easily be explained and understood in the relatively pure form in which they have thus far been proposed by the various parties.

Internal power-sharing

The objective of most forms of internal power-sharing is to guarantee an effective share in government for representatives of both major communities without eliminating the ability of the electorate to vote for a change of government. Maintaining an acceptable balance between demands for communal representation and for democratic space, however, is not always as straightforward as it sounds.

The simplest method of guaranteeing representatives of both communities a place in executive government is to provide for the allocation of ministerial positions on a strictly proportional basis between all the major parties. In Northern Ireland proportional government of this kind would mean, on present voting trends, that an executive or cabinet of ten would be made up of three or four Official Unionists, two or three Democratic Unionists, one Alliance, two or three SDLP and one or two Sinn Féin ministers. Given the substantial policy differences between these parties on some, though not all, issues, it does not take a great deal of foresight to predict that it would be unlikely to lead to stable government. It would clearly not be satisfactory to permit cabinet decisions to be made by a simple majority vote, since that would allow one community to dominate the other. Nor would it be any more practicable to allow each member of the government a veto on any policy. A system of this kind also minimizes the ability of the electorate to vote for a change of government or policy, since the make-up of every government would be broadly the same.

Considerations of this kind led the British government to prescribe a more flexible system for Northern Ireland in 1973 when the first power-sharing government was being negotiated. Under the Northern Ireland Constitution Act of 1973 an Executive may be formed only if the Secretary of State for Northern Ireland is satisfied that it would 'command widespread acceptance throughout the community' (section 2), which is generally taken to mean participation by representatives from both communities. This formula, which is still in force though it has not been activated since 1974, clearly leaves a good deal to the discretion of the Secretary of State. That in itself has been a point of contention. It has been argued that it does not provide a sufficient guarantee of participation by nationalists at the highest levels of government, and from the unionist side that it binds them to power-sharing with whatever nationalist party has the ear of the British government and thus, in effect, to an SDLP veto on all issues. The Opsahl Commission, however, was prepared to go further and recommended an equal share or veto on all aspects of government for representatives of both communities.[1] A version of this approach has already been adopted in Belgium, where there is now a formal constitutional requirement that the national Council of Ministers, the Belgian cabinet, should be composed of equal numbers of Dutch- and French-speaking ministers (see Chapter 7). But that is more readily acceptable in Belgium since the major national parties draw their members from both linguistic communities. In Northern Ireland, where the main political parties are communally exclusive and the cross-communal parties are less strong, a similar formal requirement would be more difficult to operate and might even result, on a strict application of the Opsahl recommendation, in the effective exclusion of the centre parties.

Further variations on the power-sharing model have been suggested from time to time in an attempt to get round these perceived problems. The unionist parties have regularly proposed that power-sharing should be limited to the proportional allocation of chairmanships of parliamentary committees to oversee the main administrative departments.[2] But this has always been rejected by nationalist parties on the ground that it would not give them any share in executive power. Various forms of weighted majority voting have also been proposed. When James Prior, as Secretary of State for Northern Ireland, was attempting in 1982 to get agreement on what was called 'rolling devolution' – the gradual devolution of more powers to a newly elected Northern Ireland Assembly – he accepted a unionist amendment to the enabling legislation permitting a proposal for the devolution of specified powers to be made if it had the support of 70 per cent of members of the Assembly, subject to Parliamentary approval at Westminster.[3] But the provision could not in practice be activated since both the SDLP and Sinn Féin refused to take their seats in the Assembly or have anything to do with devolution on a basis which did not contain a substantial 'Irish dimension'. They were in any event opposed to the idea since it provided no guarantee that powers, once devolved, would be shared in any way. To meet this objection, it has subsequently been suggested that a weighted majority vote of Assembly members should be required both for legislation and for executive orders on matters of special concern to one or other community.[4] This means of protection against domination by a simple majority vote has been adopted in respect of constitutional amendments in many countries. In Belgium, as will be seen, a similar but more specific protection has been provided by a requirement that legislation in the national parliament on certain matters be approved not only by a two-thirds majority of those voting but also by a majority of votes in each language group.

None of these structures for sharing in government, whether by the proportional allocation of portfolios or special majority requirements, however, can provide any absolute guarantee that one or other community will not be able to sabotage the whole structure by a refusal to cooperate in essential decisions or by a total withdrawal. That awkward fact has led many proponents of sharing in government to argue that it is better to rely on less formal compromises or conventions which by their nature are more flexible and therefore less likely to cause problems as time passes and circumstances alter. The best example of this approach is the 'grand compromise' reached in Holland in 1917 under which all the main parties agreed that future governments should contain a reasonable proportion of both Protestant and Catholic ministers. This approach leaves more space for the formation of coalitions between the main parties and is arguably more responsive to the views of the electorate. In Northern Ireland there has as yet been only one limited attempt to develop an informal compromise of this kind, when in 1985 the unionist parties offered to join a power-sharing coalition with the SDLP for an initial five-year period of reconstruction. But this proposal, known as the Catherwood initiative, was made only weeks before the finalization of the Anglo-Irish Agreement and was immediately submerged in the reaction to it.

In the Anglo-Irish Agreement the two governments none the less reaffirmed their commitment to the objective of power-sharing within Northern Ireland 'on a basis which would secure widespread acceptance throughout the community', an objective which they expressly agreed could be achieved 'only with the cooperation of constitutional representatives within Northern Ireland of both traditions there' (Article 4). But neither government has as yet expressed a clear view on any of the basic questions which experience in Northern Ireland and elsewhere have raised: whether it is better to rely on an informal deal between the major parties or to make detailed formal provision for the allocation of powers; and whether they are prepared to put any pressure on the parties on either side to accept a deal on either basis. Nor is it clear whether either government really believes the constitutional parties are willing to make the compromises necessary for the sharing of power or whether the preconditions set by unionists on the removal of any constitutional claim over Northern Ireland by the Republic and by nationalists on the need for all-Ireland institutions which reflect their aspirations for Irish unity effectively preclude any lasting cooperation between them.

Externally shared authority

Those who doubt the ability of politicians in Northern Ireland to make these essential compromises have sought to develop alternative governmental structures which recognize the divergent aspirations and interests of the two main communities but are not ultimately dependent on continuing cooperation between them. The essential element in all these structures is that the British and Irish governments should share authority over Northern Ireland on behalf of the unionist and nationalist communities respectively. But there is considerable variation in the forms of joint authority that have been proposed.

The idea of shared control over Northern Ireland by Britain and the Republic of Ireland was initially suggested in the 1970s by the SDLP, using the analogy of colonial territories like the Sudan which had been jointly ruled by Britain and France under what was known as a condominium. The concept was developed and given some greater substance as one of the options proposed in the report of the New Ireland Forum in 1984. It was described as a system of 'joint authority' under which 'the London and Dublin governments would have equal responsibility for the government of Northern Ireland' so as to accord equal validity to the two traditions there and thus to reflect the reality of their divided allegiances (Para. 8.1). The precise mechanisms by which joint authority might be exercised, however, were not discussed in any detail, though some possibilities had been explored in a number of preparatory studies commissioned for the Forum. What appears to have been envisaged was a more or less permanent system of joint direct rule with a number of ministers representing the British and Irish governments, though there was a suggestion that some powers might be devolved to an elected Assembly. The financial basis for the proposed arrangement was also left somewhat vague in the Forum Report, which stated only that 'the overall level of public expenditure would be determined by the two Governments' (Para. 8.6). An economic study commissioned for the Forum, however, suggested that taxes in Northern Ireland might continue to be levied at British rates and that the bulk of the subvention to Northern Ireland would continue to be borne by Britain; the Irish contribution was to be fixed in relation to the proportion which Irish gross national product bore to British gross national product, which in the mid-1980s would have been about 4 per cent.[5]

This kind of joint authority was open to some serious objections. It was not based on any coherent democratic principles, since voters in Northern Ireland would have little or no influence on the policies of either the British or the Irish government and no provision was apparently to be made for elected representatives from Northern Ireland to play any part at all in the selection or control of the Irish government as they did at Westminster. It was not immediately obvious why the British government should be expected to concede an equal share of authority to the Irish government while continuing to pay 96 per cent of the cost of governing Northern Ireland. No clear arrangements were suggested for sharing security duties. And in any event the system was clearly going to be completely unacceptable to unionists. It does not appear to have been seriously pursued during the negotiations leading up to the Anglo-Irish Agreement in the following year, though some commentators have argued that the right of consultation granted to the Irish government under the Agreement was in effect a first step towards a form of joint authority.

The Kilbrandon model

Since the New Ireland Forum Report a number of different models of joint authority designed to meet these various defects have been proposed. The Kilbrandon Inquiry, an unofficial all-party body set up to make a considered British response to the Forum Report, suggested that Northern Ireland should be governed by a five-person executive composed of three ministers directly elected within Northern Ireland and two appointed by the British and Irish governments respectively.[6] It was argued that this would provide both the essential element of direct responsibility to the electorate and an effective guarantee against majority decisions either on legislation or executive action which would threaten the interests of either community. The two members who would be likely to be elected by unionists would require the support of at least one of the governmental appointees before they could push through any policy opposed by the representative of Northern Ireland nationalists; conversely the nationalist member and the Irish government's appointee would require the support of the British appointee before they could push through a policy opposed by the unionists. The Kilbrandon Inquiry also suggested more tentatively that the power to legislate for Northern Ireland might likewise be shared by an interparliamentary body with representatives from the British House of Commons, the Irish Dáil and from an elected Northern Ireland Assembly. The financial arrangements under which the structures might operate, however, were not discussed in any depth.

The SDLP model

A further development of this model was proposed by the SDLP during the discussion of internal structures in 'Strand 1' of the talks process in 1992, apparently with some encouragement and assistance from their political contacts in the Republic. This version envisaged that there would be a governing executive of six members, three elected in Northern Ireland, one each appointed by the British and Irish governments and a sixth member appointed by the European Commission. The direct involvement of a European representative was intended not only to reflect Northern Ireland's status as a distinctive region within an increasingly integrated Europe and the increasing shift of financial support for Northern Ireland from Britain to Europe but also to defuse any strains which might arise within an exclusively British–Irish structure of the kind proposed by the Kilbrandon Inquiry. It is not known whether this idea was discussed with or encouraged by officials within the European Commission. But, in the light of the increasingly lukewarm support in many member states for the integrative aspects of the Maastricht Treaty of Union, it seems unlikely that it would now have much prospect of securing general agreement. No European Union institution currently has the competence to undertake any direct role in the government of any part of the Union, and because there are some other regions with similar problems to those in Northern Ireland the Commission may not wish to create a precedent of this kind. French and Spanish concerns over the implications for Corsica and the Basque country would probably be sufficient to ensure that any such move made no progress.

Shared authority

The most recent and fully developed version of this approach is the proposal for 'shared authority', published in 1993 by the Institute of Public Policy Research in close association with some members of the British Labour Party.[7] This envisages that Northern Ireland would be governed by a five-member Shared Authority Council similar to that proposed by the Kilbrandon Inquiry, with both executive and legislative powers. In both respects its work would be subject to scrutiny by committees of an elected Northern Ireland Assembly which could also propose legislation. The Royal Ulster Constabulary would be absorbed into a new Northern Ireland Police Service with additional officers seconded from British police forces and the Irish Gardai. But any Irish financial contribution would be proportional to its population or gross national product in comparison with the United Kingdom. These new structures would then be entrenched into a constitution which could be amended only by a two-thirds majority in a referendum of all Northern Ireland voters, thus providing a stronger guarantee to either community than the current simple majority required for a change in constitutional status.

The drawbacks to joint authority

Like most other models for sharing all these forms of externally shared authority would probably be workable if the cooperation of all concerned could be secured. They would all provide clear institutional recognition of the dual identities and allegiances of the unionist and nationalist communities in relation to the United Kingdom and the Republic of Ireland. They would also provide some protection against breakdown in the not unlikely event of disagreement between elected unionist and nationalist representatives or a boycott by either, since the governmental representatives could maintain the process of government without them. But there are some corresponding disadvantages, both technical and political.

On a technical level there are obvious difficulties in achieving an acceptable balance between contributions and responsibilities by the British and Irish governments in respect of finance and security. The burden of continuing anything like the current level of financial subvention and security deployment would clearly be much greater in relation to the resources of the Irish government than of the British government. If the burden were allocated in terms of ability to pay measured by gross national product, as suggested by the New Ireland Forum study, the Irish government would have an equal share of power, but the British government might find it difficult to agree that the Irish government would have to contribute only a tiny proportion of the cost. On the other hand if the burden were to be allocated equally or in proportion to the balance between the unionist and nationalist communities in Northern

Ireland, the Irish government would find it difficult either to find the resources or to justify doing so in relation to expenditure on its own population. And only a small proportion would be covered by subventions from the European Union at current levels. Nor is the Irish government likely to be able or willing to deploy its defence forces in joint patrols in anything like the numbers currently deployed by the British Army, not least since they might feel vulnerable to attack from loyalist paramilitaries in many areas. A territorial division of responsibilities between the British and Irish governments would also be difficult and might add to, rather than diminish, separatist pressures. These difficulties on the security front would clearly be much less important if new joint authority structures were being introduced with general consent. They would become much more significant if they were to be imposed in the face of general opposition from the unionist community.

The political drawbacks are equally important. There is a danger that the permanent involvement of British and Irish representatives in all governmental decisions might encourage rather than help to diminish confrontational attitudes by the elected Northern Ireland representatives, since there would be no pressing need to build and maintain the kind of cooperation over the whole range of governmental policies that is required for coalition government. And the greater the involvement of external governmental representatives in the day-to-day business of administration, the more difficult it might be to persuade the electorate that they had any real democratic control over the policies to be adopted for Northern Ireland. There might also be difficulties for the British and Irish representatives in agreeing policies for Northern Ireland which clashed with their respective domestic policies and commitments in Britain and the rest of Ireland. There are strong arguments, as suggested below, for the view that direct involvement by the two governments in the internal administration of Northern Ireland, within whatever financial resources were made available, should be regarded as an ultimate protection against discriminatory or unfair policies rather than a regular part of the processes of government. The most significant disadvantage, however, may be the continuing resistance by the major unionist parties to any direct involvement by the Irish government in internal Northern Ireland affairs. If the objective of developing new structures for the government of Northern Ireland is to encourage cooperation between the Northern Ireland parties, it may not be wise to begin by making provision for the Irish government to have a permanent place in any administration.

Compromise models

These structures for internal power-sharing and for externally shared authority are not mutually exclusive. If the objective is to maximize democratic space and accountability for politicians within Northern Ireland without jeopardizing effective protection against one-sided policies or boycotts, it may be necessary to combine elements of both in any package deal.

One way of achieving this would be to make a formal distinction between powers which may best be exercised under internal power-sharing structures and those which may be thought to require some external involvement. It may be suggested, for example, that communally sensitive matters, such as security and the administration of justice, and matters on which the British and, under some forms of joint authority, the Irish governments would have a direct interest, such as relations with the European Union and the provision of resources for public expenditure in Northern Ireland, should be reserved for a body on which there would be permanent representation from the two governments, leaving all other matters to be dealt with under formal or informal structures for internal power-sharing. This approach is implicit in the provisions for devolution under the Anglo-Irish Agreement in that the remit of the

Anglo-Irish Ministerial Conference is formally restricted to matters which have not been devolved. If any form of externally shared authority is to be developed it might conveniently be built on the existing structures for the Ministerial Conference with added provision for participation by elected representatives from the Northern Ireland parties.

An alternative approach would be to provide for external joint intervention only in cases where internal power-sharing has broken down, for example, where the members of a power-sharing executive representing one community seek to impose their will on those representing another. It would be possible in such cases for a reference to be made to a superior body such as the Anglo-Irish Ministerial Conference with power to review the issue or to impose its own decision. This might be thought of as an extended form of judicial review under which decisions alleged to be discriminatory or unfair to one or other community might be challenged. The difficulty with a purely judicial review in cases of this kind is that judges are reluctant either to formulate or to impose their own views on essentially political matters. There would be no such difficulty if, after a court decision on whether the proposed action was discriminatory, the matter could be referred to a jointly constituted intergovernmental council. That council would then have the function of resolving the dispute in the light of the court decision. The concept of a superior political body having the power to act in default when another fails or refuses to do so within the law is well established in both British and Irish law. During the prolonged withdrawal of cooperation by unionist-controlled district councils in the aftermath of the Anglo-Irish Agreement, British ministers had to use default powers of this kind to set district rates in Belfast. A similar mechanism has been incorporated in the new Belgian constitution under which a majority of either language group in the National Assembly may refer a proposed decision or law which adversely affects their interests for reconsideration by the council of ministers (see Chapter 7).

The right to be Irish

If direct participation by the Irish government in the administration of Northern Ireland were to be limited in this way – or ruled out altogether – it would be all the more necessary to provide some further recognition of the Irish identity and allegiance of nationalists in Northern Ireland on an individual level, as recommended by the Opsahl Commission.[8] One possibility, proposed by the Standing Advisory Commission on Human Rights for Northern Ireland, would be to give formal recognition to the existence of two communities by imposing a statutory duty on all public bodies to give equal treatment and esteem to members of both the Protestant/unionist and the Catholic/nationalist traditions.[9] Any complaints could then be dealt with in the usual way by court action or through the Ombudsman. Another would be to make express provision in Northern Ireland law for those who wished to assert and register their Irish identity and citizenship. Ancillary provision could then be made under parallel Irish legislation for the Irish government to provide consular and other appropriate services to such persons within Northern Ireland.

Local government and public services

Whatever structures are adopted for shared decision making at regional level, additional provision may be required to encourage sharing at lower levels of government and in other public services. If sharing rather than separation is to become a reality throughout Northern Ireland, some action will be required to reverse or stem the pressures towards communal separation in housing, education and other spheres that have been described in Chapter 2 and to give greater weight to the aspirations of the people who want to live peacefully together.

The current structures for local government and the delivery of public services such as education and health are based on the very different assumption that, since locally elected representatives of the major political parties are unlikely to agree on the delivery of public services, the functions of district councils should be cut down to the minimum. The popular comment that the only real power of district councils in Northern Ireland is over rubbish collection, leisure facilities for the unemployed and the burial of the dead is not that far from the truth. Instead the British government has developed a complex network of appointed boards and agencies to administer such essential public services as health, education, housing and the police. At a technical level most of these boards have worked reasonably well and have generally eliminated discriminatory practices in the delivery of services, notably in respect of public sector housing, though not always in their employment patterns. But they are far from democratic. Their members are supposed to be representative of both communities. But the popular perception that they are selected primarily for their willingness to implement British government policies, not least on privatization, may likewise not be far from the truth. The exclusion of elected representatives from most of the important work of administering public services cannot reasonably be claimed to have contributed much to fostering concepts of shared democratic responsibility.[10]

This continuing democratic deficit can be largely explained in terms of what is known as the 'Macrory gap' – the fact that the absence of an elected regional executive and parliamentary assembly since the collapse of the power-sharing executive in 1974 has left a gap in the governmental structures envisaged in the official Macrory Report in 1972.[11] A corresponding increase in the powers of district councils has long been one of the principal demands of the major unionist parties, though others have been wary of giving more powers to councils, not least Belfast City Council, which have continued to act in an exclusive and sectarian manner.

Incentives for sharing

Even if a new power-sharing executive and assembly can be established, a good case can also be made for encouraging the sharing of powers and responsibilities at district council level. One way of doing this would be to provide for those councils which agreed to operate in accordance with an approved code of practice to receive additional funds and to exercise a wider range of powers, notably some of those currently exercised by civil servants, such as local planning regulation, or by appointed boards, such as library services. The code of practice could include such matters as the rotation of the positions of mayor or council chairperson, committee chairs and nominations to joint boards between the major parties and appropriately weighted majority voting on issues of particular communal concern. A number of district councils, notably those effectively controlled by SDLP members, have already adopted some of these practices. But there is currently no practical incentive for others to follow or develop their example.

Incentives to encourage sharing and integration in other spheres might also be developed. Considerable efforts have been made to encourage the integration of members of the two communities in places of work. Under the Fair Employment Acts all but the smallest employers are required to monitor the composition of their workforces and, though there is no formal quota system, they are expected to take steps to remedy any significant imbalance in the proportions of Protestants and Catholics employed compared with their numbers in the relevant catchment area. There are no equivalent policies or incentives in respect of integration in education or housing.

Integrated education

Some moves have recently been made to facilitate integrated education in response to clear evidence of parental demand both from opinion polls and from the opening of new privately funded schools.[12] Under the Education Reform (NI) Order 1989 the Department of Education is now required to support the development of integrated education and to provide funds for integrated schools likely to be attended by reasonable numbers of Protestants and Catholics. But there is no duty on the Department or on education and library boards, which own and control most state schools, to ensure that sufficient integrated schools are available at both primary and secondary level to meet demand for them or to encourage the transformation of existing schools to integrated status. In practice, new integrated schools can be recognized and funded only where a sufficient number of parents are prepared on their own initiative to establish one and demonstrate its viability. In doing so they face considerable difficulties, especially at secondary level, since they are prevented from competing directly with the established selective grammar schools. For example, Lagan College, the first and largest integrated secondary school, has recently been formally prohibited from taking the ability of applicants into account in any way so as to enable it to develop more effective sixth-form provision. There are also problems in some areas in maintaining a reasonable balance in the numbers of Protestant, Catholic and other pupils in integrated schools. Under the 'open enrolment' policy, developed by the Conservative government in Britain and imposed with only minor amendments in Northern Ireland, all schools are now required to admit all applicants up to their numbers limit without consideration of their religion. The general effect is to strengthen the position of the established and largely segregated state/Protestant and Catholic sectors in continuing to provide for 'their people' and to make it difficult in many areas for a real choice of integrated schools to be offered to those parents who want them.

The provision of a range of integrated schools of all types throughout Northern Ireland to meet parental demand would require the government to face up to the entrenched interests of the churches and embark on a major reorganization with at least the kind of determination which it has displayed in respect of discrimination in employment. It would also require some amendments to anti-discrimination legislation of the kind which have already been granted to the established segregated sectors.

Residential integration

There are similar problems in respect of integration in public sector housing estates. The report on discrimination in housing provision commissioned by the Standing Advisory Commission on Human Rights in 1987 reported that the current allocation policies of the Northern Ireland Housing Executive tended to exacerbate the tendencies towards segregated housing.[13] This finding was given further support by a survey of tenant opinion by the Executive in 1989 and by a number of submissions to the Opsahl Commission.[14] The Standing Advisory Commission has already recommended that the Executive should be exempted from the strict application of anti-discrimination law in cases where that was necessary to maintain the integrated character of a particular estate or area.[15] The recommendation has been ignored. The Opsahl Commissioners also recommended that determined action should be taken by the Executive to ensure that integrated public sector housing is available for those who want it.[16] Though this is not likely to be easy in areas where there is actual or feared intimidation, it is not impossible with the combined support of tenants, the police

and other agencies. But as with integration in education it will require more than purely facilitative action by all those concerned.

Policing

Equally difficult problems are likely to arise in achieving greater
communal integration in the police and other security forces.
Though the RUC is formally committed to achieving balanced
recruitment, the twin forces of intimidation and alienation have
prevented much progress towards this objective. Some activists
and commentators, as indicated in Chapter 1, have argued that
the only way of dealing with the problem is to establish an
additional police service which would be recruited from and
deployed in predominantly nationalist areas. Though this approach might assist in dealing with the associated problems of
employment, it might also contribute to further communal
separation rather than integration. Experience in other jurisdictions in dealing with difficulties in recruitment from ethnic
minorities, notably in respect of blacks in Britain, would suggest that progress in achieving better integration will require
positive and determined action within the RUC not only to
develop patterns of deployment which will make it easier for
Catholics to join an integrated force but also to eliminate any
elements of a Protestant or unionist ethos which may contribute
to the problem. One significant improvement in this connection
would be the development of closer links with the Garda
Síochána in the Republic by way of exchange of personnel and
the use of senior officers from that force as well as British
forces in dealing with disciplinary cases.

The legal framework

Structures for sharing must not only be agreed in principle by
those directly involved, they must also be implemented in a

way which inspires confidence on all sides without imposing such rigid formal requirements as to be unworkable. This raises some important issues of content and form. How are special provisions for sharing within Northern Ireland to be related to the general constitutional framework of the United Kingdom and of the Republic of Ireland? How can conflicts with the individual rights guaranteed for all by the European Convention on Human Rights be avoided? And how can agreed provisions be effectively entrenched against change without consultation or agreement by future British and Irish governments with different ideas on what should be done? Neither unionists nor nationalists can be expected to make realistic compromises now – whether by accepting an Irish dimension to a settlement or by agreeing to join in internal governmental structures for Northern Ireland – if they fear that they may be used by the other side to demand more concessions a few years hence. It is the job of constitutional lawyers to provide answers to these questions. But they must be answers which other people can understand and trust.

Constitutional, individual and communal rights

There is unlikely to be much difficulty in making formal provision for whatever system of shared government may be agreed. Northern Ireland, unlike the rest of the United Kingdom, has had a written constitution since it was created under the Government of Ireland Act 1920. Any new provisions can readily be incorporated in a new statute to amend or replace the current Northern Ireland Constitution Act 1973. This is likely also to contain whatever provision may be agreed on the contentious issue of the constitutional status of Northern Ireland to confirm or replace the current statutory guarantee that Northern Ireland shall remain part of the United Kingdom until a majority of the people voting in a border poll decide otherwise, as discussed below.

The protection of individual and communal rights may be thought to be equally straightforward. All the parties in Northern Ireland are committed to the introduction of a Bill of Rights and the British government has indicated that it will not raise any objections to this despite its opposition to the introduction of any such Bill of Rights for the rest of the United Kingdom. The simplest approach, as is often argued, would be to incorporate the European Convention on Human Rights and Fundamental Freedoms into Northern Ireland law.[17] But that may not meet all the concerns of unionists or nationalists or people in between. The European Convention guarantees a number of traditional individual civil and political rights. It is less than satisfactory or completely silent on a number of issues of particular interest to people in Northern Ireland. There is no provision on self-determination that could be invoked to protect unionists against a unilateral decision by the British government to exclude them from the United Kingdom or to grant a dominant role to the Irish government in the internal affairs of Northern Ireland. Nor is there any provision to protect nationalists from effective exclusion from the processes of government or to guarantee their rights in respect of language, educational structures or cultural expression. Nor is there any general protection for either side from economic or cultural discrimination, since the Convention outlaws discrimination only in respect of the limited list of rights and freedoms it guarantees; these do not include some key areas such as employment and the supply of goods and services. Nor is there effective control over the introduction of repressive emergency laws, since the Convention permits member states to derogate from most of the rights guaranteed in it in any emergency which threatens the life of the nation.[18] Though some of these matters are covered in other international human rights instruments, such as the UN International Covenants and the various CSCE Documents, none of these provide any effective enforcement mechanisms.

A Northern Ireland Bill of Rights

The obvious conclusion is that a Bill of Rights for Northern Ireland will have to be specially drafted to meet the particular concerns of all sections of the community. This should not be surprising. Most countries with major communal divisions have constitutions which provide specific protections for particular groups and communities.[19] These provisions must, of course, be compatible with the more general requirements of international human rights conventions. Both the United Kingdom and the Republic of Ireland are bound by the European Convention and the UN International Covenants. Neither could adopt or agree to guarantee any provision which was contrary to its obligations under these and other human rights conventions. The best approach may be to incorporate the terms of the European Convention into a new Northern Ireland Constitution with appropriate additional provisions to satisfy all groups that by agreeing to the compromises necessary for shared government they will not be risking their fundamental interests or aspirations. If the European Convention were incorporated into the law of the United Kingdom and the Republic of Ireland, as argued below, a Northern Ireland Bill of Rights need only contain the additional provisions.

Protection against discrimination

The Northern Ireland Constitution Act 1973 already contains a prohibition on discrimination by any public body on the grounds of religious belief or political opinion. This might usefully be extended to cover indirect discrimination, as recommended by the Standing Advisory Commission on Human Rights in 1990, and perhaps also to require effective legislation to be maintained against discrimination by larger employers in the private sector.[20] It would probably not be wise, however, to attempt to include such detailed provision for specific forms of monitoring and enforcement as are currently provided in Northern Ireland under the Fair Employment Acts. Provisions in a Bill of Rights or an entrenched constitutional measure should in principle be drafted in fairly general terms and allow some flexibility for governments to alter more specific legislation to meet changing circumstances. It may also be desirable to include a general exemption for measures designed to improve the position of disadvantaged groups, as in the Canadian Charter on Rights and Freedoms, or to encourage greater integration of the two main communities, notably in education and housing. Without some form of exemption for positive measures of this kind a general constitutional prohibition on discrimination may, for example, prevent employers from making special efforts to recruit Catholics or Protestants to achieve a better balance in their workforce. It may also prevent integrated schools from implementing a policy of maintaining a reasonable balance in numbers of Protestants and Catholics and make it difficult for public housing authorities to maintain the balance of numbers in an integrated estate or development

Communal rights

Measures against discrimination, however effective, may not always be sufficient to protect the interests of communities as opposed to individuals. Non-discriminatory systems for publicly funded education or for the funding of cultural or linguistic activities may in practice increase the difficulties faced by communities in maintaining and developing their particular cultural heritage. This is now generally recognized in international human rights law. The International Covenant on Civil and Political Rights completed in 1966 was the first to include a specific provision on communal rights:

In those states in which ethnic, religious or linguistic minorities exist persons belonging to such minorities shall not be denied the right, in community with the other members of their group, to enjoy their own culture, to profess and practise their own religion and to use their own language. (Art. 27)

More recent documents, such as the *UN Declaration on the Rights of Persons belonging to National, Ethnic, Religious and Linguistic Minorities*, the *European Charter for Regional or Minority Languages* and the *Document of the Copenhagen Meeting of the CSCE*, have stressed the positive obligation of states to minorities of all kinds. The Standing Advisory Commission on Human Rights for Northern Ireland has already recommended that the Northern Ireland Constitution Act should be amended to impose a specific duty on all public bodies to give equal treatment and esteem to the two major communities in Northern Ireland.[21] In the context of a new constitution or Bill of Rights for Northern Ireland the formulations in these international instruments could be used to give more specific protection for denominational educational systems for those parents who wish them and for publicly funded support for Irish as well as British culture and language.

Emergency laws

The derogation provisions of the European Convention on Human Rights, as they have been interpreted at Strasbourg, mean that many of the general human rights guarantees can be of limited value during a conflict of the kind which has persisted in Northern Ireland since 1969. Though it would be hoped on all sides that a new settlement would bring peace, no one can reasonably rule out the possibility that serious paramilitary violence on one side or the other might continue or re-emerge and threaten the stability of any new arrangements.

Neither the British nor the Irish government is likely to be willing to abandon all possibility of introducing some emergency legislation to deal with this potential situation. And yet members of both communities would want to have some guarantee that oppressive measures could not be introduced or operated in a one-sided or abusive way. One possible approach to this might be to make provision in a new constitution or Bill of Rights for additional safeguards, such as a weighted majority in a Northern Ireland Assembly or the joint consent of both the British and Irish governments, as a condition for the declaration of any state of emergency or the introduction of particular emergency powers. It may also be helpful in this context to make explicit provision for the involvement of international monitors on the introduction or operation of any emergency powers, for example, by making use of the new procedures for missions of experts agreed at the Moscow Meeting of the CSCE, as discussed in greater detail in Chapter 8.

Entrenchment

The underlying problem in respect of the entrenchment of any Bill of Rights or equivalent constitutional guarantees for Northern Ireland is the prevailing view that under the unwritten British constitution Parliament may repeal any prior legislation by a subsequent statute. It follows that either a Bill of Rights or a new Northern Ireland Constitution Act with extended guarantees of individual or communal rights could be repealed by any subsequent Act of Parliament and would thus provide no lasting guarantee. There is an additional political difficulty in that the current British government does not favour the adoption of any entrenched Bill of Rights or written constitution for the United Kingdom as a whole and might, therefore, be likely to oppose any form of entrenchment for Northern Ireland that could be used as a precedent by proponents of a

British Bill of Rights or a written constitution. It may be possible, however, to surmount these difficulties by relying on mechanisms which are specific to Northern Ireland and do not set such a precedent.

The simplest approach would be to follow the precedent of the Government of Ireland Act 1920 by limiting a Bill of Rights to those matters which had been devolved to a Northern Ireland Executive or Assembly. But that would not cover matters reserved to the United Kingdom government or Parliament. And any new constitution or Bill of Rights for Northern Ireland enacted in that way would in any event be subject to repeal by any future Act of Parliament. If a new Northern Ireland Constitution or Bill of Rights had in addition been endorsed by a local referendum it could be argued that it would thereby achieve a special status and could not properly be repealed without the consent of the people of Northern Ireland. There is no clear legal authority for such a proposition, however, and it would not inspire much confidence in those who are suspicious of British intentions.

A better approach may be to rely on some form of external entrenchment under international law. If the terms of a new Northern Ireland Constitution or Bill of Rights were incorporated into a new British–Irish Agreement, any subsequent amendment or repeal without the consent of both governments would be a breach of the treaty which could be challenged through the International Court of Justice.[22] This would not, of course, prevent subsequent British and Irish governments acting together to alter or abandon the terms of the treaty and might not, therefore, satisfy those unionists and nationalists who are suspicious of the long-term commitment of either government on the status of Northern Ireland. An alternative approach which might engender greater confidence on both sides would be to involve the Council of Europe as a guarantor of any new settlement, as discussed in greater detail in Chapter 8.

Enforcement

Similar issues may arise over procedures for the enforcement of any new constitution or Bill of Rights. A purely internal system of adjudication, through a specially constituted Constitutional Court for Northern Ireland, may not be thought by all to carry sufficient weight or to be wholly independent. An appeal to an exclusively British court, such as the House of Lords or the Judicial Committee of the Privy Council, is likely to be equally unacceptable to nationalists, given the record of the British courts in dealing with cases arising from Northern Ireland. A joint British–Irish Court might be more acceptable to national-ists and would clearly be more appropriate if the constitution or Bill of Rights were incorporated in a new British–Irish Agreement. It might also be possible to arrange for the involve-ment of one or more judges from the European Court of Human Rights, on the model envisaged for the protection of minority rights in Bosnia under the original Vance–Owen peace plan, as explained in Chapter 8.

North–South relations

There are two principal objectives in developing new structures for relations between Northern Ireland and the Republic of Ireland: the economic and the political. The economic objective is to improve the economic performance and prosperity of both parts of Ireland by mutual cooperation. The political objective is to assist in the process of achieving peace and stability in Northern Ireland and in Ireland as a whole.

The case for the development of better economic cooperation between the two parts of Ireland is easy to make. The political divisions since the introduction of partition in the 1920s have resulted in a much lower level of trade and general economic

integration between North and South than might otherwise
have been expected (see Chapter 5). The infrastructure for
transport and other forms of communication, both physical
and personal, was similarly neglected. Northern Ireland developed a high degree of integration and dependency on the rest
of the United Kingdom. The Republic sought first in the 1930s
to pursue a policy of economic self-sufficiency and when this
was abandoned in the 1960s it developed links with Europe
and America with a view to lessening its continuing dependence
on Britain. In recent years a good deal of progress has been
made in rebuilding economic and infra-structural links under
the programmes for cross-border cooperation sponsored by the
European Union and the detailed programme of intergovernmental work on cross-border issues initiated under the Anglo-
Irish Agreement. But there is general agreement in the business
community that there is scope for further cooperation and
development in North–South trade within the framework of
the single European market in such areas as the supply of
components and services, integrated marketing and distribution, financial services, specialized education and training, and
the improvement of the transport and communications infra-
structures necessary to such developments.[23]

Cross-border institutions

All this would clearly benefit from the creation of cross-border
institutions, whether on a voluntary or an official basis, to
promote cooperation and ensure that full advantage is taken of
European Union schemes for cross-border development. There
is also scope for the development of cross-border institutions in
such areas as tourism, state aid for industrial development and
agriculture. But there also appears to be general agreement in
the business community that it is best, wherever possible, to
pursue this kind of cooperation on a strictly non-political basis.

The development of formal institutions for economic or other forms of cooperation between Northern Ireland and the Republic none the less has a political dimension that cannot realistically be ignored. From a unionist perspective the most acceptable form of cooperation is one in which each side enters into whatever institutional arrangements seem most appropriate on an equal and reciprocal basis. The model most frequently referred to in this context is that of the Foyle Fisheries Commission which was established in 1952 to purchase from the Irish Society the fishing rights in the estuary of the River Foyle, through which the border between Northern Ireland and the Irish Republic passes, and to regulate future fishing on a joint North–South basis.[24] The Commission is composed of two representatives each from the Northern Ireland and the Irish governments and has the power to make legally enforceable regulations, subject to separate parliamentary approval in both jurisdictions, on all aspects of fishing and related activities. This model was explicitly referred to by the Ulster Unionist Party in its proposals for joint North–South bodies to deal with matters of mutual interest during the 'Strand 2' talks in Dublin in 1992. Its attraction for unionists is that it places the representatives of Northern Ireland on an equal footing with those of the Republic and has no implications of any kind in respect of Irish unification.

From a nationalist perspective there is a clear preference for the development of institutions with authority over the whole of Ireland on specified matters. The model most frequently referred to is that of the Council of Ireland which was provided for in the Government of Ireland Act 1920 and proposed again in the Sunningdale Agreement of 1973, although it was never actually established. The Council would have had executive authority over a range of matters in the economic and environmental spheres and also in the control of certain aspects of policing. But its main function would have been to assist in the harmonization and coordination of laws and administrative systems in both parts of Ireland. The attraction of this approach to nationalists is clearly that it emphasizes the value and legitimacy of institutions based on the principle of Irish unity. The need for all-Ireland institutions with executive powers was repeatedly stressed by the SDLP and the Irish government during 'Strand 2' of the talks process in 1992.

How can these two opposing positions be reconciled within the framework of structures for sharing? As with most other structures for sharing, both are in principle acceptable and workable provided all the parties involved are willing to work them. That in itself suggests that it may be better for those who aspire to the development of shared arrangements for the whole of Ireland not to insist on institutions which assert or imply any form of Irish unification but to agree to the principle of mutual recognition and reciprocity in the ceding of certain functions to an all-Ireland body. This is more likely to lead to the development of enduring institutions which make a practical contribution to economic and environmental cooperation than an attempt to impose a political blueprint. Experience in the European Community and elsewhere has shown that moves towards economic and other forms of cooperation between independent jurisdictions are most likely to succeed if they are developed on a pragmatic and gradual basis rather than with a pre-arranged agenda. Those who aspire to Irish unification by consent would do well to follow the example of the founders of the European Community who established a framework for greater European unity through economic institutions in the 1950s and 1960s on an open-ended basis.

One of the most important contributions to such a process on the part of the Republic of Ireland will be the amendment of the initial articles of the Irish Constitution, which makes claims on behalf of the Irish people and state which are unacceptable to unionists precisely because they deny to the people of Northern Ireland the right to make such decisions for themselves.[25] In the Downing Street Declaration the

Taoiseach, Albert Reynolds, acknowledged 'the presence in the Irish Constitution of elements which are deeply resented by Northern Unionists'. A possible reformulation of these articles is discussed in Chapter 8.

British–Irish relations

A similar approach may be taken to the development of structures for relations between Britain and Ireland. The primary objective and obligation of the British government, as stated in the Joint Declaration of December 1993, is to facilitate whatever arrangements the politicians and people of Northern Ireland and the Republic wish to develop for relations between North and South. The role of the Irish government, as one of the parties to that relationship, cannot be quite so detached. But there is scope for the development of structures for relations between the Republic and Britain which will assist rather than hinder cooperative relations within Ireland.

In the initial stages the existing relationship between the two governments established under the Anglo-Irish Agreement of 1985 is to be continued, as stated in the Joint Declaration. But there is clearly scope for change and development in those structures as new relations between North and South are developed. The Anglo-Irish Agreement itself made express provision for the functions of the Anglo-Irish Ministerial Conference to be reduced as alternative governmental arrangements were developed within Northern Ireland and between North and South. A new British–Irish Agreement to supersede or replace the 1985 Agreement, as has frequently been demanded by unionists and offered by both the British and Irish governments, should be designed to reflect the developing relationships between all parts of Britain and Ireland.[26]

One way of achieving this would be to detach the Anglo-Irish Intergovernmental Council and Ministerial Conference from its current almost exclusive focus on Northern Ireland and make it a forum for continuing relations between the United Kingdom as a whole and the Republic of Ireland. This would involve expanding the competence both of the ministerial conference and of the parliamentary tier, the Anglo-Irish Interparliamentary Body, to all aspects of British–Irish relations, including such issues as the control of all forms of serious crime and terrorism, immigration and emigration, and cultural cooperation. The Interparliamentary Body might then be given stronger powers, equivalent to those of the parliamentary committees which now operate in both jurisdictions, to monitor the performance of both governments in relevant areas.

In time, provision might be made for the representation on a new British–Irish Intergovernmental Council of this kind not only of the government of Northern Ireland but also of whatever regional governmental structures may be established in Scotland and Wales. The ultimate objective, if this approach were followed, would be to create a new British–Irish Council on the model of the Nordic Council, through which political, economic and cultural relationships between Denmark, Sweden, Norway and Iceland have been channelled since the 1950s.[27] The historical relationships between those countries were scarcely less complex and coloured by warfare and domination than those between England, Scotland, Wales and the two parts of Ireland. New and more accommodating structures reflecting current governmental arrangements as well as the different status of each of these historic and modern jurisdictions could play a significant role in developing new and more appropriate relationships between them within the framework of the European Union.

CHAPTER 7

Structures for Separation

If it proves impossible to secure sufficient agreement on workable structures for sharing, the best alternative may be separation. This can scarcely be regarded as a particularly satisfactory outcome. But it may be preferable to indefinite communal conflict. In a marriage there may come a point when it is better to recognize that those involved cannot realistically be expected to go on living together in a state of perpetual conflict, but must make sensible and practical arrangements to live apart. So too, if the Protestant and Catholic communities in Northern Ireland cannot agree to workable arrangements for living together, it may be better to develop structures under which they can live in relative peace with each other by minimizing contact between them. It is sometimes said that good fences make good neighbours. In a similar way communal separation may sometimes lead to better community relations.

It does not follow that there must be a new partition under which a much smaller and more exclusive Protestant Northern Ireland would be created for the unionist community. The distribution of Protestants and Catholics and others throughout Northern Ireland, as explained in Chapter 2, would make that very difficult to achieve without major population transfers. There are other much less disruptive ways in which two distinctive communities in a single territory may organize their government and essential public services without requiring much direct cooperation between them. One possibility, which might be called the cantonal system, is to divide the territory into a large number of administrative units in such a way that maximum numbers in the two communities can live with and be governed by their own representatives and institutions. Another, which might be called functional separation, is to create a range of separate institutions for the delivery of as many public services as possible, such as education, health and welfare, on a communal basis without drawing rigid territorial boundaries.

Systems of this kind have been developed in other divided societies as a means of allowing distinctive communities to live peacefully apart within the same national framework. Switzerland, with a population of only six and a half million, is divided into no fewer than twenty-two self-governing cantons. The recently revised Belgian Constitution makes detailed provision for the allocation of functions between the French-speaking and Dutch-speaking communities, both on a regional and a functional basis. Northern Ireland is not the same as either Switzerland or Belgium. But if the search for agreement on structures for sharing is unsuccessful, examples of structures in other countries which have successfully accommodated separation may assist in the development of equivalent structures for Northern Ireland. Both cantonal and functional separation, however, are dependent on the creation of effective system for cooperation in the allocation of resources and other central or regional functions. If even that level of sharing cannot be achieved, the pressures towards even more complete separation by way of a formal repartition might become irresistible.

Cantonal separation

The essence of cantonal separation is the creation of as many units of local administration as are necessary to enable most people to live within a relatively homogeneous communal unit. As many powers and responsibilities as is practicable would then be devolved to those communal cantons, leaving only essential regional or national decisions to be dealt with at higher levels.

The best known example of this kind of structure is Switzerland. The Swiss population is divided into three or four major linguistic groups – German, French, Italian and Romansh – and also by religion.[1] The various combinations of language and religion are accommodated in twenty-two self-governing cantons, some of which have a total population of fewer than 100,000. Though each is territorially distinct, in some places the boundaries have been drawn or altered to take account of small pockets of the relevant linguistic or communal group which may be separated from larger settlements. Many of the systems of internal cantonal government are rooted in history. But most involve a mixture of elected representatives and popular referendums on specific issues. A similar mixture of representative democracy and popular voting was built into the confederal constitution developed during the nineteenth century. The federal council, which sits in Berne, now exercises an increasing range of governmental functions in respect of such matters as defence, foreign relations and national taxation. But the cantons retain substantial powers in respect of local legislation, taxation and services and their representatives have specific blocking powers at federal level.

It would not be impossible to develop an equivalent system of local government in Northern Ireland with boundaries designed to reflect the patterns of communal separation described in Chapter 2. The most obvious example would be the creation of a new unit of local government for Catholic areas in West and North Belfast. It might also be possible to create new units to reflect some predominantly Protestant enclaves on the east bank of the Foyle in Derry, in Fermanagh and Tyrone and in the Kilkeel area of South Down, and the predominantly Catholic enclave in northeast Antrim. But it would probably be impractical to draw boundaries to reflect the highly fragmented pattern of communal separation in most medium-sized and

small towns and in many rural areas. In these areas and at a
regional level there would still be a need for workable structures
for the sharing of power and the allocation of resources by
representatives of both communities. Redrawing local government boundaries could help to diminish conflicts between the
communities and to increase the extent to which people in
both communities could participate in effective decision making
on matters of popular concern in some areas. But it cannot
realistically be proposed as a general solution.

Functional separation

An alternative approach to the development of separate institutions for the two communities would be to allocate powers
and resources on a functional rather than a purely territorial
basis. This would involve establishing a series of communal
bodies or institutions, which might be either elected or appointed, to organize appropriate public services exclusively or
primarily for members of one or other community.

Education is the most obvious example. A Catholic Maintained Schools Council, fully funded by the government, has
already been established to administer and supervise central
services for Catholic schools in Northern Ireland. A similar
non-statutory body, the Northern Ireland Council for Integrated Education, is also funded by the government, though on
a much less generous basis, to assist in the development and
supervision of integrated schools. It would clearly be possible
to extend this type of structure to all schools. There has
already been some pressure from the Protestant churches in the
context of a proposed reorganization of educational administration for the creation of an equivalent Protestant Schools Council to replace the cross-communal education and library boards
which currently fund and control all state schools, most of
which are effectively Protestant. The result would be that all

schools would be under the exclusive control of bodies which represented the Catholic, Protestant or 'integrated' communities rather than of cross-communal bodies. The Catholic Maintained Schools Council is an appointed body, under the control of the Catholic bishops. But there would be nothing to prevent the organization of elections by parents at Catholic, Protestant and integrated schools to give the system a more democratic foundation. Elected Catholic and Protestant School Boards have been in operation in parts of Quebec for more than a century, with powers not only to provide schools for their communities but also to levy local taxes to pay for them.

The concept of providing essential public services through communally based institutions rather than on a strictly territorial basis could readily be extended to other spheres. Health and welfare services would be an obvious example. Though most families choose to go to doctors from their own community, health centres, hospitals and welfare services are administered on a cross-communal basis by appointed boards and trusts. But there is already some *de facto* separation in social work. Many social workers prefer and are permitted or encouraged to work with members of their own community. It would be relatively easy to formalize this and to establish separate boards, perhaps with some elected members, to provide all personal social and welfare services on a communal basis. Extending this to hospital services would be more difficult, given the policy of centralization in large regional all-purpose hospitals that has been pursued since the 1970s. But it would be possible to revert to more explicit communal provision in some areas, notably West Belfast, by detaching the Catholic-founded Mater Hospital from the control of the cross-communal Eastern Health and Social Services Board and developing it as an all-purpose hospital for Catholics in the Belfast area.

Governmental support for cultural and recreational activities could also be restructured on a communal basis. This would involve the development of separate bodies for the administration of public funds for the arts, for sports and for leisure facilities, each of which would then receive a proportional allocation of available resources from the central administration. Since many cultural and sporting activities are already highly segregated, this would not be particularly difficult and might, as in Belgium, be an effective means of giving members of each community a feeling that they were in effective control of their own cultural and recreational identity. Provision might also be made for separate Irish-language or mixed-language television and radio channels for the nationalist community, leaving the BBC to cater primarily for the unionist community.

The Belgian example

Recent constitutional and administrative developments in Belgium provide the most useful and directly relevant example of the creation of structures for communal separation.[2] Though the particular circumstances are, as always, very different, experience in Belgium shows how provision for communal separation within a unitary democratic state which lies at the very heart of the European Union can be developed to accommodate different communal identities and aspirations.

Belgium, like Northern Ireland, is a deeply divided society which was created by historical circumstances rather than any very strong feeling of national identity. The northern part of the country is populated by the Flemings, who speak Dutch and are overwhelmingly Catholic. The southern part is populated by the Walloons, who speak French and have a tendency towards secular rather than Catholic values. The capital city of Brussels lies just inside Flemish territory but was historically dominated by a French-speaking political élite. In the nineteenth century the French-speakers in Brussels and the heavily industrialized parts of Wallonia were the more prosperous and politically dominant community. The upper classes in Flanders also spoke French. Despite the long and distinguished history of towns such as Antwerp, Bruges and Ghent, the Dutch-speaking Flemings were generally treated as a less-developed and essentially agricultural community. As the twentieth century progressed, however, the Flemings began to demand a greater share in political power and there were increasing communal strains, not least over the use of Dutch for education and official purposes. Since 1945, the Flemish community has grown rapidly in relative numbers and prosperity, not least as a result of the Common Agricultural Policy and the development of new industries, while the Walloon community has suffered in both respects from the decline of its basic industries of coal mining and iron and steel making. By the late 1980s, the population of the Flemish region at 5.7 million was almost double that of the Walloon region at 3.2 million, with a further 1.0 million in Brussels. The gross national product of the Flemish region was slightly higher than the European Community average while that of the Walloon region was similar to that of Northern Ireland at just over 80 per cent of the average.

This rapid change in the relative position of the two communities caused considerable political difficulties and occasional public disorders. The Flemish national party grew rapidly at the expense of the nationally organized Christian Democrats, Socialists and Liberals and demanded greater recognition and autonomy for Flemings. The result, worked out in a lengthy process of constitutional reform over a period of more than thirty years, has been an increasing degree of separation between the two communities. As shown in Map 7.1, Belgium is now divided into three main regions, Flanders, Wallonia and Brussels, each of which has a large degree of autonomy (Article 107quater).[3] There are also four language regions: the Dutch-language region, the French-language region, the bilingual region of Brussels and a small German-language region (Article 3bis). Finally, there are three officially recognized communities,

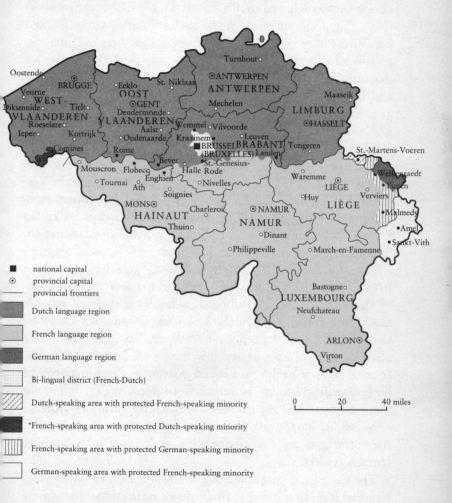

Map 7.1 *Linguistic areas of Belgium*

the Flemish community, the French community and the German-speaking community (Article 3ter). In Flanders and Wallonia all publicly funded education and most official business is now conducted exclusively in Dutch and French respectively. In addition, two separate Communal Councils and Executives have been created with specific powers over matters of special concern to Dutch and French speakers throughout Belgium; these councils have exclusive jurisdiction over cultural and linguistic matters, and most aspects of education (Article 59bis). These various institutional reforms have been introduced gradually throughout the 1980s.

This division of functions has since 1989 been replicated within the Brussels region, where about 80 per cent of the people speak French and only 20 per cent speak Dutch. The governing Council and Executive is divided into three overlapping sections – a French Community Commission, a Flemish Community Commission and a Joint Community Commission. The elected representatives on the French and Flemish Community Commissions sit separately and have exclusive jurisdiction over educational, cultural and personal matters for their communities. There are no bilingual schools, though all schools teach both French and Dutch. The Joint Community Commission, on which all the representatives sit, has jurisdiction over all bi-communal matters, such as transport and planning and some aspects of health and social assistance. But a majority of both linguistic groups is required to approve legislation on these matters. And the exercise of executive authority requires a consensus among all four members of the joint executive, two of whom are French-speaking and two Dutch-speaking (Article 108ter).

The increasing communal separation is further reflected at national level in a number of formal constitutional provisions to guarantee a form of power-sharing and to enable the representatives of the two main communities to block measures adversely affecting their interests. The most important, as indicated in Chapter 6, are the requirements that with the exception of the prime minister there must be an equal number of Flemish and French speakers in the national Council of Ministers, the Belgian cabinet (Article 86bis), and that a three-quarters majority of the elected representatives of each language group in the national assembly may vote to refer back to the Council of Ministers any law or executive decision which they feel threatens good relations between the communities (Article 38bis). Finally, the constitutional rights of each community are entrenched by a provision requiring any relevant constitutional amendment to be approved both by a majority of each language group in each house of the National Assembly (provided also that a majority of each group is present) and by two-thirds of the total votes cast (Article 1).

The relevance of the Belgian example for Northern Ireland

No one could sensibly argue that these highly complex arrangements in Belgium could be directly copied to provide recognition and protection for the two main communities in Northern Ireland. The point of setting them out is much simpler: to show that structures for communal separation can be developed and that they are both workable and respectable. The legislation requiring public education in Dutch- and French-speaking areas in Belgium to be conducted in Dutch and French respectively were challenged as an abuse of the human rights of those who wished to be educated in their own language. But in the *Belgian Linguistics Case* they were upheld by the Commission and Court of Human Rights at Strasbourg as reasonably necessary to protect the interests of the two main communities.[4]

There are, however, some significant differences between the situation in Belgium and the situation in Northern Ireland which require some further discussion. The most important is that the two communities in Northern Ireland are much more closely intermingled than those in Belgium, with the result that most of the structures developed in Belgium on the basis of territorial separation would be difficult to apply. The structures based on functional separation, notably those applied in the mixed linguistic and communal area of Brussels, may be a more useful source for ideas. But the concept of functional separation raises some awkward problems in respect of two of the most contentious communal issues in Northern Ireland, those of policing and of fair employment.

Problems of policing

It is relatively easy to develop separate structures for policing where there is a clear territorial separation between two or more communities. Each district or canton could recruit its own local police force, as in Switzerland. Alternatively, two or more larger regional forces recruited on a communal basis could provide policing for predominantly Catholic or Protestant districts or cantons. On either basis it would be possible to provide employment for some ex-paramilitaries in appropriate areas as reserves or auxiliaries and thus to ease their transition from communal self-defence to communal policing. The incorporation of previously outlawed paramilitary activists in the forces of the state is a standard and usually effective means, along with an amnesty for past offences, of establishing an acceptable basis for the restoration of law and order. It was adopted in both the Irish Free State and Northern Ireland in the 1920s. Nor would either of these approaches exclude the maintenance of a single superior force with powers to deal with specified matters, such as terrorist activity or traffic offences for the whole of Northern Ireland. A distinction between locally or regionally organized police and a national

gendarmerie is well established in many European jurisdictions.

It would be more difficult to provide for distinctive communal policing within a functional separation system. It would
certainly not be easy to maintain two parallel police forces
with potentially competing jurisdiction throughout Northern
Ireland. Nor would it be easy to secure the acceptance of
republican paramilitaries even as auxiliaries in a single police
force for the whole of Northern Ireland which was based on
the existing Royal Ulster Constabulary. The best approach
might be to arrange for the deployment in appropriate areas
on an informal basis of predominantly Catholic or Protestant
units from as representative a force as can be established. If
policing on a strictly communal basis is a prerequisite of a
lasting settlement, then some form of territorial separation is
probably unavoidable.

Problems of fair employment

The natural implication of a system of government in which
each community looks after its own affairs is that each would
be permitted to employ its own people in its own public
services. The same expectation would presumably extend to
most small- and medium-sized businesses. This would not be
easy to reconcile with the kind of fair employment legislation
which currently applies in Northern Ireland, under which all
major employers are expected to achieve a reasonable balance
between the two communities in their workforces. It may be
significant in this context that while there is a general prohibition against discrimination on the basis of race or religion in
the Belgian Constitution, there is no system of anti-discrimination legislation in respect of employment, either in the public
or private sectors. In Flemish and Walloon areas, public bodies
and employers are expected to look after their own, and even

in the bilingual Brussels region there is no requirement of balance in communally run services or in private employment. The only bodies which are expected to maintain a reasonable communal balance are those public bodies which operate at a national level and large private companies which likewise operate on a national basis.

The development of structures for separation in Northern Ireland would thus be likely to involve some significant changes in the Fair Employment Acts. The most important would be the exemption of a much wider range of employers from the obligation not to discriminate on the grounds of religion and to monitor their workforces with a view to eliminating any impediments to achieving a reasonable balance. An exemption of this kind has always been made in respect of teachers to permit Catholic schools to give preference to Catholic teachers, and other schools to other teachers, if they so wish.[5] A similar exemption would presumably be required for other publicly funded bodies whose functions were directed exclusively at one or other community. Exemption might also have to be granted to voluntary bodies and private employers operating in communally distinctive areas or spheres. The impact of fair employment legislation might then be limited to public bodies with responsibilities for the whole of Northern Ireland and perhaps also to major private employers operating throughout Northern Ireland, though they might be permitted to seek an overall balance in all their operations rather than in each individual workplace.

It is difficult to predict what the effect of such a limitation of the fair employment legislation might be. It is possible, given the established commercial strength of the Protestant community and the somewhat higher birthrate in the Catholic community, that it would increase rather than diminish the problems of differential employment and unemployment rates among Catholics. This was certainly what happened during the period of unionist rule and also until recently under direct rule. The experience in Belgium, however, has been that the rapidly increasing Flemish community has prospered, if not at the expense of, at least in comparison with the Walloon community, which has seen many of its basic industries fall into decline. It would, in effect, be left to the members of each community, and those between, to rely on their own initiative and entrepreneurial skills and to enjoy or suffer the consequences of greater or lesser economic success.

A model for Northern Ireland?

These various considerations suggest that if structures for greater communal separation are to be adopted in Northern Ireland a mixture of territorial and functional separation would provide the most acceptable compromise.

The first requirement would be to redraw local government boundaries in such a way as to create as many relatively self-contained areas as is practicable in which the population would be overwhelmingly Protestant or Catholic. This would probably involve the creation of a new local government district for West Belfast and parts of North Belfast, the separation of the east and west bank parts of London/Derry, and perhaps also the alteration of the boundaries of Moyle District Council and some others to increase the level of communal homogeneity. In other districts where this was not practicable, certain areas might be formally or informally designated as of one or other community and local services would be organized and controlled in such a way as to reflect this.

In addition throughout Northern Ireland major public services, such as education, health and social services and recreational and cultural facilities and support, would be functionally separated so that members of each major community, including those who wished for integration, would be able to choose schools, hospitals and leisure services which were designed

206 Northern Ireland: The Choice

primarily for them and for which they would be expected to pay separate taxes or rates. As has already been explained, this kind of functional separation has long been established in education and the principle of communal self-administration has recently been formalized by the creation of the Catholic Maintained Schools Council. This principle could readily be extended to the reorganization of the health and social services and education and library boards that has already been embarked on.

The need for communal cooperation and sharing would in such a system be limited to essential regional services, such as the administration of justice, certain aspects of security and policing and the raising and allocation of financial resources. Ideally this would be carried out by an elected power-sharing assembly and executive, which as in Belgium might be divided into separate communal chambers for certain functions, notably the exercise of powers of veto on any legislative or executive decisions which were discriminatory or threatened the essential interests of any major community. But it would also be possible for these central functions to be carried out, in default of agreement on a workable system of power-sharing, by a joint or shared authority council on which the British and Irish governments would be directly represented.

If intercommunal violence can be effectively controlled and eventually eliminated, whether by a voluntary peace process or otherwise, there is no reason why structures of this kind could not be maintained indefinitely. If it continues, however, it is more likely that the process of territorial separation would continue and that some form of repartition would eventually become unavoidable.

Relations with Ireland and Britain

The nature of the relationships between a communally separated Northern Ireland and the British and Irish governments would depend largely on the structures of communal separation which were adopted. But the divergent loyalties of the two main communities would almost certainly result in a tendency for the Catholic and Protestant communities to seek to develop closer working relationships and institutions with the Irish and British governments respectively. There would thus be an inherent tendency in any system of communal separation towards some form of joint or shared British–Irish authority over Northern Ireland and for the recognition of its special status within the European Union.

The various models of joint authority set out in Chapter 6 could in principle be adapted to meet whatever form of separation was agreed between the two communities. One immediate consequence would probably be closer relations between the nationalist community and the Republic. Initially, Northern nationalists might be granted a right to elect representatives to the Oireachtas, the Irish parliament.[6] Such a right could be additional to the right to vote and stand for any Northern Ireland assembly and the Westminster parliament. This might lead in some areas to association or merger with the Republic. Relations between the Republic and unionist-controlled parts of Northern Ireland, which would presumably wish to strengthen their links with British institutions, would be likely to be limited to essential economic cooperation governed by the requirements of the European Union. In such circumstances the traditional ideal of Irish unification would become highly remote.

CHAPTER 8

Getting There

Almost any of the alternatives outlined above for communal sharing or separation in Northern Ireland would in principle be workable. The real problem lies in achieving sufficient agreement among unionists and nationalists on a set of structures to make them work. In this sense the process of getting there is at least as important as the choice between the particular measures in themselves. The objective is not simply to find the fairest and most effective structures for governing Northern Ireland. It is to find a way of securing sufficient agreement on one of the various possible options to allow it to be established and maintained in the face of almost certain opposition from some people on one side or other or both.

This raises yet another set of questions. Is the 'peace first' strategy which the two governments embarked on in the Downing Street Declaration really likely to assist in achieving a maximum level of agreement, or is it likely to drag on for so long or to involve so many concessions to the IRA that overall agreement will become less likely? Is the alternative of abandoning all further discussion or contact with the IRA or Sinn Féin and continuing with the talks process while the paramilitaries continue with their respective campaigns any more likely to produce agreement on future structures, or should the two governments simply press ahead and implement what seem to them to be the fairest and most workable structures? And is there any way in which the people of Northern Ireland can be directly involved in the process of determining their own future government?

The preferred strategy of the British government until it was persuaded to join the Irish government in the Downing Street Declaration was to continue with the interparty talks which were started in 1992, in the hope that peace would follow a settlement between the major constitutional parties. This was also the strategy of the Irish government until the completion of the Hume–Adams dialogue in September 1993; since then the Irish government has been openly pursuing a 'peace first' approach, in the hope that if a lasting cessation of violence by the IRA could be achieved by some development of the Hume–Adams proposals then a political settlement would be more easily agreed. There is still some scepticism, however, on whether the four main parties, with or without the involvement of Sinn Féin, will be able to reach a sufficient consensus to enable any new structures to be put into operation. Many commentators have argued that the two governments – or the British government acting alone – will ultimately have to produce and impose a settlement. Others, like Initiative '92 and the Opsahl Commission, have argued that ordinary people should be given a greater role, by referendum or otherwise, in deciding on possible approaches to a settlement rather than merely in ratifying a deal between the political parties.

The choice of any of these approaches – seeking an end to violence as the first priority, continuing with party talks, imposing a settlement agreed by the two governments and relying on popular referendums – is, of course, likely to affect the way in which the various parties and the people react to particular proposals. The choice of strategy may in practice influence, if not determine, the ultimate outcome. A preference for a particular outcome may likewise set some limits on the available strategies. If the ultimate objective is sharing, as stated in the Anglo-Irish Agreement of 1985 though not explicitly in the Downing Street Declaration of December 1993, there must be a strong presumption that it is better to proceed by seeking agreement than by attempting to impose a package, however reasonable it may be in the abstract.

The issue of self-determination

The choice of strategy is also closely linked to the issue of self-determination. Though the Opsahl Commission stressed the dangers which may stem from competing claims to self-determination in divided societies,[1] the issue cannot be ignored. Differences over the concept of self-determination are clearly part of the problem in Northern Ireland: nationalists tend to assert a right of self-determination for the Irish people as a whole while unionists assert a separate right for the people of Northern Ireland to determine their own political status. The concept of self-determination in one form or another also forms part of most of the current proposals for a settlement. An acceptance of self-determination for the people of Ireland linked to that of consent by unionists to any new structures is an essential part of the Hume–Adams plan for peace. The concept is also a key component in the Downing Street Declaration of December 1993 in which the British government agreed 'that it is for the people of the island of Ireland alone, by agreement between the two parts respectively, to exercise their right of self-determination on the basis of consent, freely and concurrently given, North and South, to bring about a united Ireland, if that is their wish'. This complex and carefully balanced formulation raises yet more questions. What does self-determination mean in law? What might it mean in practice? And can the concept really be used to facilitate a settlement?

The right to self-determination is built into the United Nations International Covenants in the following terms:

All peoples have the right to self-determination. By virtue of that right they freely determine their political status and freely pursue their economic, social and cultural development.

An earlier conception of the same idea is built into Article 1 of the Irish Constitution:

The Irish nation hereby affirms its inalienable, indefeasible, and sovereign right to choose its own form of Government, to determine its relations with other nations, and to develop its life, political, economic and cultural, in accordance with its own genius and traditions.

What amounts to a qualified right of self-determination for the people of Northern Ireland, however, is also built into the Northern Ireland Constitution Act and recognized in Article 1 of the Anglo-Irish Agreement.

These conflicting claims have been one of the mainstays of the current IRA campaign. The IRA seeks to justify its armed struggle against the British presence in Ireland by the assertion that the right of the people of Ireland to self-determination was frustrated by the partition of Ireland in the 1920s and by the terms of the Northern Ireland Constitution Act and that this right to self-determination must be recognized before there can be peace. The question whether this interpretation is justifiable, legally or politically, was the central issue in the prolonged dialogue between the SDLP and Sinn Féin in 1988 and the more recent talks between John Hume and Gerry Adams. The corresponding question, whether the right of self-determination can properly be exercised by the people of Northern Ireland and the Republic separately or concurrently, is likewise a crucial issue in the interpretation of the Downing Street Declaration. Is there any correct answer to these questions in international law?

It is generally accepted by international lawyers that the right to self-determination can be validly asserted not only by the formation of a separate independent state but also by integration in or association with another state. That poses no difficulty either for unionists or nationalists. The real problem is the identification of what constitutes a people. The generally accepted criteria are:

1 A distinctive identity in terms of such matters as language, culture or religion

2 A shared history

3 Association with a particular territory

4 A communal commitment to assert or maintain a distinctive identity or status[2]

Almost the same set of criteria with the possible exception of 3, however, are accepted for the identification of a minority which does not have a right to self-determination but only a right to be recognized and to have some control over its own government. The most developed formulation of this is in the *Declaration on the Rights of Persons belonging to National, Ethnic, Religious and Linguistic Minorities* recently adopted by the General Assembly of the United Nations:

Persons belonging to minorities have the right to participate effectively in decisions on the national and, where appropriate, regional level concerning the minority to which they belong or the region in which they live, in a manner not incompatible with national legislation. (Art. 2(3))

Similar wording was adopted in 1990 in the Copenhagen Document of the CSCE, in which both the British and Irish governments participated.

The essential problem is that both major communities in Northern Ireland – or in Ireland – have an arguable case for treatment either as a people or as a minority.[3] In this sense the Opsahl Commission was right to stress the dangers which may arise from undue concentration on self-determination in a place like Northern Ireland. One possible resolution of these competing claims, however, may be found in the view of some human rights lawyers that the right to self-determination and the rights of a minority to be recognized and to have some control over their own government merge into each other. It ought to be possible to find an acceptable form of words based on the formulation in the Downing Street Declaration and on relevant international documents which would meet the claims of both major communities in Northern Ireland in this respect.

This could then be incorporated into a Bill of Rights, which would form part of a new Northern Ireland Constitution, and also into an amended Irish Constitution.

Which unit for self-determination?

This approach would not resolve the more difficult problem of whether each community in Northern Ireland, the people of Northern Ireland, or the people of Ireland as a whole are to be the unit of self-determination. The idea that any settlement should be approved by both communities in Northern Ireland in separate votes is initially attractive and was given some support in the Opsahl Report.[4] But it would create difficult problems in identifying who was entitled to vote in which community and what should be done with the people in between. A better way of ensuring general cross-communal support would be to set a minimum threshhold of the order of 65 per cent to 75 per cent to validate any proposal.[5] In any case, both the British and the Irish governments, as has been seen, have committed themselves in the Anglo-Irish Agreement to accepting that it is the people of Northern Ireland as a whole who have a right to determine their constitutional status. But Sinn Féin and the IRA appear to be committed to the view that any decision must be made by the Irish people as a whole. One of the key elements in the Hume–Adams peace plan seems to be a proposal to deal with this impasse by holding a dual referendum in Northern Ireland and the Republic, so that both Sinn Féin and the IRA could honourably call off their campaign of violence in response to a vote by the Irish people as a whole. The idea is a good one. But its political value depends entirely on the kind of questions that are asked. Any suggestion that a dual referendum could be used in effect to ensure a majority for nationalists over unionists would clearly be unacceptable. It would, however, be possible to involve the people in the Republic of Ireland in the process of reaching a settlement, the basis of which had been worked out by the parties to the talks process or through an advisory referendum of the kind suggested below. The fact that a referendum is required in the Republic to make any change in its constitution provides an ideal opportunity for an exercise of this kind. If identical wording is used in relevant articles of a new Northern Ireland Constitution and in parallel amendments to the Irish Constitution a dual referendum would be entirely appropriate. If it also assisted the IRA and other paramilitaries to cease their armed campaigns, that would be a strong argument for pursuing it as a practical means of achieving a peaceful settlement. But none of this can in practice be done until agreement of some kind has been reached. The question of how any agreement is to be reached between all those involved must be resolved before there can be any formal act of self-determination.

The 'peace-first' strategy

The idea that the first priority in seeking a political settlement in Northern Ireland should be to secure peace is obviously attractive. It ought to be easier to secure agreement on a compromise if the threat of serious paramilitary violence and the heightened communal tension which it brings with it can be removed. The ceasefire proclaimed by loyalist paramilitaries in the initial stages of the talks process in 1992 was widely welcomed on these grounds. And following the discussions on the Hume–Adams proposals in September 1993 the Irish government apparently accepted the validity of a 'peace first' approach and persuaded the British government to give it a try. The result was the Downing Street Declaration of December 1993 (see Chapter 4).

At the time of writing the final response of Sinn Féin and the

IRA had yet to be given. But even if it is initially favourable there must be some caution about the longer-term merits of this line of argument. One problem is that an offer of peace from the paramilitaries on one side may not be reciprocated by the other. The IRA did not respond in any positive way to the loyalist ceasefire in 1992. And the immediate reaction of the loyalist paramilitaries to the Hume–Adams proposals was to increase rather than decrease the intensity of their campaign against what they viewed as a pan-nationalist conspiracy. The underlying problem is that paramilitaries tend to represent the most uncompromising attitudes within their communities and that the conditions or 'price' for a ceasefire or cessation of their campaigns are likely to be unacceptable either to their counterparts on the other side or to the major political parties. Both the loyalist paramilitaries and the unionist parties have made it clear that they are completely opposed to the granting of any role for the Irish government in the internal affairs of Northern Ireland, which seems likely to be a precondition for any settlement acceptable to Sinn Féin, if not to the SDLP. In addition, an essential element in the Hume–Adams proposals appears to be not only a declaration by the British government that it has no long-term interest in retaining Northern Ireland as part of the United Kingdom, but also that it should undertake to 'join the persuaders' and take active steps to convince the unionists of the merits of Irish unification, which would amount to a denial of their fundamental commitments. The refusal of the British government to include any such undertaking in the Downing Street Declaration has posed major problems for Sinn Féin and the republican movement.

There is the further problem that the offer of peace by the IRA under the Hume–Adams proposals, like the ceasefire during talks by the loyalists in 1992, appears to be based on the assumption that a compromise agreement will actually be achievable in the ensuing talks process. It is not clear what the reaction of the IRA would be if the continuing talks process or even an all-Ireland conference which also appears to be part of the Hume–Adams plan failed to reach agreement within the parameters set by their proposals. The threat that in such circumstances the armed struggle would be resumed by the IRA, as it was by the loyalists in 1992, cannot be ignored. It is certainly unrealistic to expect the paramilitaries on either side to abandon all possibility of a resumption of their campaigns in defence of their fundamental commitments before the basis of a general settlement becomes clear. Undue concentration on achieving 'peace first', without some indication that a settlement acceptable both to the IRA and Sinn Féin and to the major political parties will be achievable within a reasonable period, may raise unrealistic expectations that a lasting peace can be achieved quickly. And in practice it may be difficult to do that without the kind of direct negotiations with the paramilitaries which the two governments have consistently ruled out in advance of a cessation of violence.

Negotiating a settlement with the parties

The main argument for continuing to seek consensus among the major parties on a new settlement appears to be that new structures for sharing can only work if the leaders of the main parties have agreed to them in advance. There is some force to this. Over the past twenty years a number of initiatives designed to re-establish devolved government in Northern Ireland on a shared basis have been thwarted by the refusal of one side or the other to cooperate in any way: between 1982 and 1985 James Prior's proposal for 'rolling devolution' was effectively vetoed by the refusal of both the SDLP and Sinn Féin to take up their seats in the Northern Ireland Assembly; after 1985, the refusal of the main unionist parties to cooperate in any way with the structures set up under the Anglo-Irish Agreement prevented any real progress towards the objective of greater cooperation between the two communities in the processes of government.

There is also some support from political scientists, notably in the work of Arend Lijphart, for the view that power-sharing in a divided society is most likely to be delivered through a compromise settlement made by political leaders strong enough to lead their communities in that direction. But here too there are some difficulties.[6] Lijphart's list of preconditions for successful power-sharing, referred to as 'consociation' by political scientists, includes a number of factors not obviously present in Northern Ireland, such as a high level of cross-communal linkages in non-political spheres, a measure of cross-communal support for the main political parties and the existence of a strong political élite able to survive in the face of pressures towards absolutist positions from their communities. The account of the two communities in Chapter 2 suggests that in Northern Ireland there is a low level of cross-communal linkages in most spheres of activity and very little cross-communal support for the major political parties. The capacity of the political élite to face down extremist tendencies among their voters must also be doubtful. Unionist politicians often point to the fate of Terence O'Neill and Brian Faulkner, both of whom were driven out of office by opponents of compromise within their own communities. On the nationalist side, there have been equally noticeable pressures towards the accommodation of more demanding communal aspirations, for example, by the virtual elimination of the socialist wing of the SDLP and the greater interest shown by John Hume in developing a common policy with the Dublin government and Sinn Féin than with the Official Unionist or Alliance Parties. It is often claimed by politicians in Northern Ireland that no one ever lost any votes by adopting uncompromising communal positions. The failure of the repeated initiatives by successive British governments designed to achieve agreement among party leaders on shared structures for government certainly seems to suggest that, if Lijphart's analysis is correct, there is little prospect of success in continuing to rely exclusively on inter-party talks as a means of achieving agreement.

Imposing a settlement

Despair over the prospects of achieving a workable settlement in inter-party talks has led other commentators to advocate the imposition of a compromise settlement by the two govern-ments. Though this approach is theoretically open in respect of any package, in practice it is usually advocated in respect of one or other form of externally shared authority. If the primary objective is some form of internal power-sharing, it is difficult to see how the major parties on either side can be forced to cooperate with an imposed package. There is also a danger that an attempt to impose some form of settlement, notably one which involved a substantial role for the Irish government in the internal affairs of Northern Ireland or one which sought to integrate Northern Ireland with the rest of the United Kingdom without any recognition of an Irish dimension, would result in a substantial hardening of attitudes within the unionist or nationalist communities and thus to an escalation in paramili-tary activity. It would probably be possible for the two govern-ments to maintain structures for joint authority in the face of this kind of reaction. But the prospect of an indefinite continua-tion of loyalist violence and the increasing separation of the two communities which it would be likely to cause may not be one which the two governments would wish to risk.

Sanctions?

An alternative way of seeking to secure agreement on a compro-mise settlement would be to threaten or impose financial or economic sanctions on those who refused to cooperate. It has often been claimed that too many people in Northern Ireland, particularly those in the public sector and the professions who are living comfortable lives unaffected by the conflict but heavily subsidized by the British Exchequer, have opted out of the political process and have been unwilling to countenance or encourage any form of political compromise. The British government could make it clear that continuing financial support for Northern Ireland would be dependent on acceptance of a meaningful Irish dimension to any future structures for government.

Economic sanctions by all accounts had a salutary effect on the business and professional community in South Africa and helped to create a climate of opinion in the white community which made possible the ending of apartheid and the negotiation of a multi-racial democracy. A similar strategy in respect of American investment in Northern Ireland pursued by Irish–American groups under the banner of the McBride Principles, despite opposition from the British government, played a part in securing greater acceptance for the introduction of stronger anti-discrimination laws in the late 1980s. Economic sanctions directed against the more prosperous sections of the community might have a similar effect in Northern Ireland. One specific proposal which has recently been made is that a security tax should be levied in Northern Ireland to pay for compensation for bomb damage and other security expenditure so that everyone in Northern Ireland, and particularly the better off, would feel more directly the real cost of a continuation of the conflict.[7]

There is a danger, however, that sanctions of this kind would merely convince the unionist community that a comprehensive 'sell-out' was underway and would increase the level of support for paramilitary activity on the loyalist side. Thus far both governments have avoided any attempt to rely on sanctions of any kind and they would not fit well with the general strategy of the Downing Street Declaration which emphasizes the need for consent and agreement. If this fails, the case for some form of economic sanction would be more difficult to dismiss.

The referendum strategy

The argument for involving the population at large in the process of seeking a compromise is based on the proposition that there is a greater willingness to compromise among large sections of both communities than among their political leaders. This runs counter to the analysis of the preconditions for successful power-sharing by Lijphart and others. But there is some evidence from the hearings of the Opsahl Commission and from recent opinion polls, as set out in Chapter 2, that it may be true. If it is, the two governments should be able to harness sufficient popular support for a package deal to make it difficult either for party leaders to refuse to cooperate with it or for paramilitaries to continue to oppose it. Both the IRA and loyalist paramilitaries claim repeatedly to be acting on behalf of the Irish or the Ulster people and clear evidence in a referendum that a majority in both communities supported a particular settlement would destroy that claim. It would be particularly difficult for the SDLP and Sinn Féin to oppose such a result, provided it was endorsed by an equivalent majority in the Republic of Ireland.

This strategy has not as yet been tried in Northern Ireland, not least because of the reluctance of the British government to set more precedents for decision-making by popular referendums in the context of the continuing arguments over membership of the European Union. The only occasion on which a referendum has been used during the current conflict was in the 'border poll' in 1973. On that occasion it was used as a means of resolving the basic constitutional status of Northern

Ireland for the time being before proceeding to elections for a new Northern Ireland Assembly and the ensuing talks about the composition of a power-sharing executive. But there is not much support for repeating that exercise now, not least because any such border poll would almost certainly be boycotted by most nationalists as it was in 1973. Since 1973, the people in Northern Ireland have been involved in the process of seeking a settlement only through the choice of party representatives in the normal round of Westminster, Assembly and district council elections.

The idea of combining democracy by popular referendums with that of representative democracy, as exemplified in the inter-party talks process, is clearly somewhat unfamiliar in a British context, though it was used in 1979 to establish the degree of popular support for devolution to Scotland and Wales. The potential and practicalities of this strategy will therefore be discussed at somewhat greater length, drawing on experience in some other comparable jurisdictions, notably that of Newfoundland in the late 1940s.

The Newfoundland example

In the 1940s Newfoundland faced many of the problems which currently face Northern Ireland.[8] Since 1855 it had been a self-governing British colony. But following a financial crisis in the 1930s direct rule from Westminster, through an appointed Commission, had been imposed and Newfoundland remained economically dependent on Britain. Though there was no intercommunal conflict, the Protestant and Catholic sections of the population were clearly recognizable and had somewhat different aspirations. Immediately after the war a Constitutional Convention was elected to consider possible future forms of government. The main choices were to continue as a British colony, to move to full independence as a separate country, and to seek confederation with Canada, or even with the United States. After two years of complex negotiations the Convention voted by a clear majority to put two options to the people of Newfoundland in a referendum: to restore responsible government as it had been before 1934 as a self-governing colony, or to continue for five years with the current system of government by commission. This provoked a sustained campaign by those who favoured confederation with Canada, led by a prominent Orangeman, Joseph Smallwood, culminating in a mass petition to the British government requesting that the option of confederation should be included in the referendum. This was eventually agreed, with the consent of the Canadian government, and the referendum was held in 1948 on the three options. In the first ballot 45 per cent voted for responsible government, 41 per cent for confederation and 14 per cent for government by commission. In a second ballot held shortly after, from which the option of government by commission was excluded, however, there was a clear though small majority for confederation (52 per cent) over responsible government (48 per cent). Despite worries over the opposition of the Catholic hierarchy to confederation, the vote of the majority of the electorate was accepted and implemented.

The implications of experience in Newfoundland in the 1940s for Northern Ireland in the 1990s are not so much in the outcome as in the procedure adopted for getting there. It shows clearly the potential of a referendum procedure which does not merely ask for a Yes or No vote on a prearranged package, but puts a range of realistic options to the electorate. A referendum procedure may be used in this way as an aid to establishing what is the most acceptable compromise as well as legitimating the final outcome. It also shows the importance of the way in which the range of options to be put to the electorate is drawn up. If the choice of options is left to negotiations between the parties or governments involved, the people may not be presented with what is in reality the most popular compromise, since each party or government is likely to press for what it perceives to be the most desirable outcome from its own political perspective rather than the one most likely to achieve overall consensus. In Newfoundland it took a sustained political campaign and a mass popular petition to achieve the inclusion of the option which eventually proved to be the most acceptable. It also shows, if that were necessary, the importance of the way in which the questions are formulated. There were lengthy negotiations between the British and Canadian governments over the precise formulation of the questions posed in the first and second Newfoundland referendums.[9]

A preferendum?

The use of an indicative referendum procedure in Northern Ireland was expressly provided for in the legislation for the Northern Ireland Constitutional Convention in 1974. This may well have been in direct reliance on the Newfoundland precedent, since it was frequently referred to in the government's discussion papers. The formal provision was as follows:

The Secretary of State may by order direct the holding of a poll or polls for the purpose of obtaining the views of the people of Northern Ireland on any matter contained in or arising out of a report of the Convention or otherwise concerned with the future government of Northern Ireland. (Northern Ireland Act 1974, section 2(3))

Though this provision lapsed when the Convention was wound up, a similar power could readily be re-enacted for use in connection with proposals arising out of the current talks process. It must be stressed, however, that an indicative referendum of this kind – sometimes referred to as a preferendum – is unlikely to be given binding force.[10] It must be clearly distinguished from a referendum to approve and legitimate a particular constitutional package or provision, as in the case of referendums held in the Republic of Ireland to approve changes to the Irish Constitution. The objective of a preferendum is to establish which of a range of realistic options is most likely to secure general popular support or acceptance rather than to find out, as in most commercial opinion polls, what are the first preferences for a wider range of options some of which are recognized to be unacceptable.

There may, therefore, be a case for a two-stage referendum procedure. First, the government would organize one or more indicative referendums in the North to clarify the type of settlement which would be likely to secure the highest level of popular support in both communities; this would be followed by more detailed discussion with the parties on the precise formulation of the necessary constitutional amendments both to the Northern Ireland Constitution Act and to the Irish Constitution; there could then be twin or successive referendums in Northern Ireland and in the Republic to ratify both new constitutional settlements, each of which would contain the same wording on key issues.

What questions to ask?

The choice of referendum questions and their precise wording is a notoriously difficult and skilful business and must be directly related to the purpose of the exercise. In the case of Northern Ireland the object of the exercise is to establish which of the realistic and potentially workable options is most likely to be acceptable to both communities and thus to lead to greater political stability. There would therefore be little point in asking questions about immediate unification or a return to simple majority rule. The analysis in Chapters 6 and 7 suggests that the effective choice is between three or four broad sets of structures, all of which assume that Northern Ireland will

remain within the United Kingdom for the foreseeable future
and that direct links of some kind will be established with the
Republic of Ireland, as laid out in the accompanying table.

Option A   Continued direct rule
The continuation of direct rule from London in consultation
with the Irish government under the terms of the Anglo-Irish
Agreement.

Option B   Power-sharing with joint North–South institutions
Government by an elected power-sharing Executive supervised
by a Northern Ireland Assembly and the creation of a number
of joint institutions with the Republic of Ireland to deal with
specified matters of mutual interest on a reciprocal basis.

Option C   Separate institutions for the two main communities
Creation of separate structures for the government of the two
main communities on a territorial or functional basis as appropriate subject to power-sharing or joint authority between the
British and Irish governments on the allocation of resources.

Option D   Joint authority
Government by a form of joint authority between the British
and Irish governments in association with an elected power-
sharing Executive and Assembly which would have responsibility for all matters on which devolution could be agreed.

Voters might then be asked to state their preference among
these broad options either by the single transferable-vote system
of proportional representation, as currently used for Assembly
and local government elections, or by successive referendums
in which the least popular options would be excluded, as in the
Newfoundland example.

It will be immediately obvious that the full details of any of the available options could not be spelled out in a ballot paper. But it would not be difficult to explain the options in greater detail in official documents circulated to all voters in advance of the referendum, as in the case of the British and Irish referendums on membership of the European Community. And if a two-stage process were adopted, it would not be necessary to fill out all the details, since the object of the exercise would be to give those responsible for drafting a constitution an indication of voters' preferences. When a new constitution had been completed, it could then be put to a further referendum for ratification within Northern Ireland along with the parallel referendum which would be required for the accompanying amendments to the Irish Constitution.

British and Irish action

Both the British and Irish governments clearly have a vital part to play in the search for peace and stability in Northern Ireland. Until the outbreak of the troubles in 1969 neither government was really interested in the problem and seemed content to lend more or less unqualified support to unionists and nationalists respectively in their mutually incompatible claims. Since then they have sought to work more closely together, notably in the periods leading to the Sunningdale Agreement in 1973 and the Anglo-Irish Agreement in 1985. But the problem of competing claims to sovereignty and the continuing pressure to lend support to 'their people' often resulted in divergent signals from London and Dublin as to the best way forward. One of the most significant and encouraging elements in the Downing Street Declaration is the recognition that it is the task of both governments, as representatives of the British and Irish people, to give effect as best they can to the wishes of the people of Northern Ireland rather than to pursue their own state or party objectives.

From the British side this shift in emphasis is reflected in a key passage of the Declaration:

The British government ... have no selfish strategic or economic interest in Northern Ireland. Their primary interest is to see peace, stability and reconciliation established by agreement among all the people who inhabit the island, and they will work together with the Irish government to achieve such an agreement, which will embrace the totality of relationships. The role of the British government will be to encourage, facilitate and enable the achievement of such agreement over a period through a process of dialogue and cooperation based on full respect for the rights and identities of both traditions in Ireland.

This amounts in practical terms to an undertaking to give effect to whatever agreement is reached by the people of Northern Ireland or their representatives with those of the Republic.

On the Irish side the undertaking is less unequivocal and is coloured by its commitment to the ideal of Irish unification. But the Taoiseach on behalf of the Irish government explicitly accepts that 'it would be wrong to attempt to impose a united Ireland, in the absence of the freely given consent of a majority of the people of Northern Ireland' and confirms that 'the Irish government will, as part of a balanced constitutional accommodation, put forward and support proposals for change in the Irish Constitution which would fully reflect the principle of consent in Northern Ireland'. In practical terms this means that the Irish government is undertaking to make whatever constitutional changes are necessary to implement a balanced constitutional package, which by clear implication includes one under which Northern Ireland remains part of the United Kingdom until the majority of its people decide otherwise.

The best way of giving formal effect to these undertakings is to translate them into the fundamental law of both states. An indication of how the current conflicting constitutional claims

Figure 8.1 *How the constitutional conflict might be handled*

Current constitutional provisions

Bunreacht na hÉireann 1937

1   The Irish nation hereby affirms its inalienable, indefeasible and sovereign right to choose its own form of government, to determine its relations with other nations and to develop its life, political, economic and cultural, in accordance with its own genius and traditions.

2   The national territory consists of the whole island of Ireland, its islands and territorial seas.

3   Pending the re-integration of the national territory, and without prejudice to the right of the Parliament and Government established by this Constitution to exercise jurisdiction over the whole of that territory, the laws enacted by that Parliament shall have the like area and extent of application as the laws of Saorstát Éireann* and the like extra-territorial effect.

   *i.e. the 26 counties of the Republic of Ireland
   **Under section 1(1) of the Irish Free State (Consequential Provisions) Act 1922 the 1920 Act applies only to Northern Ireland.

Government of Ireland Act 1920

1(2)   For the purposes of this Act, Northern Ireland shall consist of the parliamentary counties of Antrim, Armagh, Down, Fermanagh, Londonderry and Tyrone, and the parliamentary boroughs of Belfast and Londonderry.

75   Notwithstanding . . . anything contained in this Act, the supreme authority of the Parliament of the United Kingdom shall remain unaffected and undiminished over all persons, matters and things in [Northern]** Ireland and every part thereof.

Northern Ireland Constitution Act 1973

1   It is hereby declared that Northern Ireland remains part of Her Majesty's dominions and of the United Kingdom, and it is affirmed that in no event will Northern Ireland or any part of it cease to be part of Her Majesty's dominions and of the United Kingdom without the consent of the majority of the people of Northern Ireland voting in a poll held for the purposes of this section in accordance with Schedule 1 of this Act.

A possible reformulation for use in both jurisdictions

1   The territory of the island of Ireland is divided into two parts, the
State of Ireland and Northern Ireland. The State of Ireland consists of the
area over which the laws of Saorstat Éireann applied,* its islands and
territorial seas. Northern Ireland consists of the six parliamentary
counties of . . ., its islands and territorial seas. {The citizens of the State
of Ireland hereby express their aspiration to the coming together of the
people of the island of Ireland and the unification of the island by
consent and agreement of the people of both parts of Ireland.}

2   The people of the island of Ireland hereby affirm that they alone shall
have the right to choose, by agreement between the two parts respectively,
their own form or forms of government, to determine their relations with
the other part, with the United Kingdom and with other states, to
develop their natural resources and to pursue their own political,
economic and cultural traditions.

3   Northern Ireland at present forms part of the United Kingdom of
Great Britain and Northern Ireland by the wish of the greater number of
its citizens. If at any time in the future a majority both of the people of
the state of Ireland and of Northern Ireland voting freely and
democratically and without coercion in concurrent polls held in
accordance with the Schedule to this Constitution consent to the
unification of the island of Ireland or to any other constitutional
arrangement covering the whole island of Ireland the Government of [the
United Kingdom] {Ireland} shall introduce the legislation necessary to
give effect to that arrangement.

[. . .] Northern Ireland Constitution   {. . .} Irish Constitution can be reconciled, relying on the wording of the Downing Street Declaration is set out in Figure 8.1.

The Declaration is less specific on the nature of the constitutional and governmental structures which may be required. The joint governmental commitment 'to seek along with the Northern Ireland constitutional parties . . . to create institutions and structures which, while reflecting the diversity of the people of Ireland, would enable them to work together in areas of common interest' does not distinguish between what have been called here structures for sharing and structures for separation. But there is explicit reference to the need for 'institutional recognition of the special links that exist between the people of Britain and Ireland'. Again this amounts in effect to an undertaking to develop whatever institutions can be agreed to reflect the three strands of relationships identified during the talks process: the internal government of Northern Ireland, relations between Northern Ireland and the Republic and relations between Britain and Ireland. On all these matters the agenda is essentially open-ended, as indeed it should be in accordance with the principles of democracy and self-determination. The relationships between the various parts of the British–Irish Isles, including Scotland and Wales, should be allowed to develop in accordance with the wishes of their peoples without a pre-determined objective, as have those between the countries of Western Europe in the European Community and Union.

Neither government, however, can escape its underlying obligation, not least under the European Convention on Human Rights and the CSCE Documents, in the event of a failure of the parties to agree on a single set of structures to take all necessary steps to maintain an effective system of government for Northern Ireland and to protect its people from unlawful violence and both its communities from oppression by the other.

The role of external actors

There remains the question of the proper role of other countries and bodies with an interest in the resolution of the Northern Ireland problem. There have been repeated calls over the years for international diplomatic intervention and for the deployment of United Nations peace-keeping forces. More recently there has been a concerted campaign for the appointment of a United States peace envoy to assist in finding a settlement. Would such direct intervention help or hinder a settlement? And if it would hinder, what should the international community be doing to help?

The answer to these questions is that the role of the international community in general and of European bodies, such as the European Union, the Council of Europe and the CSCE, is necessarily more limited than that of the British and Irish governments. If the two governments working together cannot devise and deliver a peaceful settlement in Northern Ireland, it is unlikely that other countries or the international community could intervene to any better effect. The record of direct international mediation in deep-seated national and ethnic conflicts, such as those in the Lebanon and former Yugoslavia, is not good. The most constructive approach for interested states and international bodies may be instead to offer their good offices in encouraging, guaranteeing and monitoring a settlement achieved by the United Kingdom and the Irish Republic.

This approach can best be explained in relation to the proposal for the appointment of an American peace envoy. This idea was promoted by the Irish-American lobby during the 1992 US presidential election and was given some support by President Clinton during the campaign. Since his election, however, he has declined to pursue the idea while the British and Irish governments are actively engaged in the search for a settlement. This is the right policy. An American envoy appointed at the behest of Irish-Americans would inevitably be suspected by unionists of pursuing a nationalist agenda and would be unlikely to make any better progress in reconciling the two communities than the joint efforts of the two governments. The better role for the United States government is to give what support they can to the British and Irish governments in pursuing the current peace and talks processes and to encourage the Irish-American community to channel its legitimate concern through economic investment.

The role of the European Union in this context is likely to be similarly restricted. The European Commission has to date been reluctant to play any major political role in negotiating constitutional changes in areas of dispute between its member states. It has shown little interest in the proposal by the SDLP that it should nominate a commissioner to share the government of Northern Ireland with nominees of the British and Irish governments and three locally elected representatives. Nor is there much prospect in the immediate future, while the European Union remains an association of states, of the recognition of Northern Ireland, or any other similarly disputed frontier zone, as a region with special status outside the territory of any one member state. It would be formally possible for the European Union to guarantee a new British–Irish Agreement by becoming a party to it or by accepting it as a protocol to the Treaty of Rome or the Maastricht Treaty of Union, but this too might be seen as too dangerous a precedent to be acceptable. Its most constructive contribution may be the recognition of Northern Ireland as a special border region and the provision of appropriate financial and economic support.

The Council of Europe may be able to play a more active role in helping to guarantee and adjudicate on the individual and communal rights aspects of any new settlement. It appears to be generally accepted that formal adjudication on human rights issues should be left to the Commission and Court of Human Rights at Strasbourg rather than taken over by the

European Union or any newly constituted body. As has been seen, the creation of a special court with representatives from the Commission and Court in Strasbourg to adjudicate on individual and communal rights in Bosnia was informally approved by the relevant Council of Europe institutions as part of the Vance–Owen plan for Bosnia. Though that particular proposal has been overtaken by events, the precedent could be built on in the context of a new British–Irish Agreement over Northern Ireland. Some form of recognition by the Council of Europe of the terms of the human rights elements in a new Agreement, and the possibility of referring disputes to an independent external adjudicatory body distinct from the British and Irish courts, might assist in giving confidence to both sides in Northern Ireland on the validity of any individual and communal rights provision in a new British–Irish Agreement.

The developing institutions of the Conference for Security and Cooperation in Europe (CSCE) may be able to assist in a similar way, not least since in some respects, notably on the protection of minorities, its procedures are more developed and specific than those of the Council of Europe. The Copenhagen Document of 1990 sets out a number of significant principles of particular relevance to Northern Ireland: that 'persons belonging to national minorities have the right freely to express, preserve and develop their ethnic, cultural, linguistic or religious identity and to maintain and develop their culture in all its aspects, free of any attempts at assimilation against their will'; that there may be a need for 'special measures' to ensure full equality for members of minorities; and that minority communities have the right to establish educational and cultural institutions within the state and contacts with common communities across national frontiers, and to effective participation in national affairs. Though the CSCE process does not provide for any formal adjudication on these matters, it does provide under the so-called Vienna and Moscow mechanisms for diplomatic intervention by participating states and for the appointment of missions of experts to visit and report on the situation in territories in which there are human rights concerns. In addition, under the Helsinki Decisions of 1992, a High Commissioner for Minorities has been appointed to monitor the performance of participating states on the treatment of minorities.[11]

These monitoring systems could be used to provide additional international safeguards against any continuing human rights abuses by security forces and to ensure that the Copenhagen principles on minority rights were being effectively adhered to in any new settlement in Northern Ireland. Some positive action may be necessary, however, to make this possible. The British government entered a reservation to the Moscow mechanism to the effect that it might on security grounds refuse to allow a mission of experts to visit particular areas. And the terms of reference for the High Commissioner for Minorities specifically exclude any intervention in situations involving terrorism. It would clearly be desirable as a means of generating confidence in a new settlement for Northern Ireland if it could be agreed that international monitoring under the CSCE process would be accepted without reservation both in respect of minority protections and human rights generally.

The ultimate step in international intervention would be the deployment of a European or United Nations peace-keeping force. But the precedents for direct military intervention of this kind are not encouraging. If there was no agreement between the British and Irish governments or the major parties in Northern Ireland as to its future government, the promise or actual deployment of an international peace-keeping force in place of the British Army would merely be a signal to the nationalist and loyalist paramilitaries that the time for serious fighting over territory had arrived.

Notes

CHAPTER I **Separation or Sharing**

General reading

Some of the issues in this chapter are discussed at greater length in F. Boal and N. Douglas (eds.), *Integration and Division* (1982). Some specific examples of countries in which structures for sharing have been successfully implemented are given in a recent Minority Rights Group Pamphlet, Claire Palley *et al.*, *Minorities and Autonomy in Western Europe* (1991). For a discussion of the developing international law on self-determination and the rights of minorities see Hurst Hannum, *Autonomy, Sovereignty and Self-Determination: The Accommodation of Conflicting Rights* (1990) and Patrick Thornberry, *International Law and the Rights of Minorities* (1991).

References

1. Community Relations Commission, *Flight* (1972).

2. Raymond Murray, 'Hunt for an Alternative', *Fortnight*, Issue 316 (1993).

3. For a general discussion of the development of integrated schools in Northern Ireland see Chris Moffat (ed.), *Education Together for a Change* (1993).

4. The most detailed statement of CSCE policy on minorities is in the *Copenhagen Document of the CSCE* (1990).

CHAPTER 2   **The Two Communities and the People in Between**

General reading

The best and most accessible history of the plantation of Ulster and its later impact is Roy Foster's *Modern Ireland 1600–1972* (1988); see also A. T. Q. Stewart, *The Narrow Ground: Aspects of Ulster 1609–1969* (1977).

References

1. John Whyte, *Interpreting Northern Ireland* (1990).

2. Gerry Adams, *A Pathway to Peace* (1988).

3. Simon Lee, 'Lost for Words', *Fortnight*, Issue 316 (1993).

4. Andrew Boyd, *Holy War in Belfast* (1969).

5. Gillian Robinson, *Cross-Community Marriage in Northern Ireland* (1992), p. 11.

6. This way of looking at Northern Ireland was first developed by Frank Wright in *Northern Ireland: A Comparative Analysis* (1988).

7. Robert Cormack *et al.*, *The Higher Education Demand Survey* (1989).

8. The latest statistics indicate that in the lowest age group of children aged from nought to five years the numbers of Protestants and Catholics are now equal, while previously there was a majority of Catholics in that age group.

9. Paul Compton, 'The Demographic Background', in D. Watt (ed.), *The Constitution of Northern Ireland: Problems and Prospects* (1981).

10. Northern Ireland Housing Executive Research Unit, *Public Attitudes Survey* (1990), Table 5.

11. Ibid., Figure 7.

12. David Smith and Gerry Chambers, *Equality and Inequality in*

Northern Ireland 4: Public Housing, Policy Studies Institute Occasional Paper 47 (1989), pp. 57–8; *A Citizens' Inquiry: The Opsahl Report on Northern Ireland* (1993), Chapter 10, para. 3.7.

13. See generally John Sugden and Alan Bairner, *Sport, Sectarianism and Society in a Divided Ireland* (1993).

14. Seamus Dunn, 'A Short History of Education in Northern Ireland 1920–1990', *Fifteenth Annual Report of the Standing Advisory Commission on Human Rights for 1989–90* (1990), HC 459, Annex B.

15. Seamus Dunn and Ed Cairns, 'A survey of Parental Opinion on Education in Northern Ireland', *Seventeenth Annual Report of the Standing Advisory Commission on Human Rights for 1991–92* (1992), HC 54, Annex I.

16. For a general review of issues and statistics on discrimination in employment see the report of the Standing Advisory Commission on Human Rights, *Report on Fair Employment* (1987), Cm 237.

17. Fair Employment Commission, *Summary of the 1992 Monitoring Returns* (1993), p. 116.

18. Ibid., p. 8.

19. For a more detailed discussion on these issues see the recent research study carried out for the Joseph Rowntree Foundation, *Catholic–Protestant Income Differences in Northern Ireland*, obtainable from Professor Vani Borooah, University of Ulster.

20. John Whyte, *Interpreting Northern Ireland* (1990), p. 73.

21. Roger Jowell *et al.*, *British Social Attitudes: the 7th Report* (1990).

22. Eddie Moxon-Brown, *Northern Ireland Attitude Survey* (1978); David Smith, *Equality and Inequality in Northern Ireland: Part 3: Perceptions and Views*, Policy Studies Institute Occasional Paper 39 (1987).

23. Report of a poll on the recommendations of the Opsahl Commission, *Fortnight*, Issue 320 (1993).

24. See note 21.

CHAPTER 3   The Armed Struggle

General reading

A good up-to-date account of the conflict is Brendan O'Brien, *The Long War* (1993). The best general accounts of the IRA are Tim Pat Coogan, *The IRA* (1980), John Bowyer Bell's *The Secret Army*, 4th ed. (1989) and Patrick Bishop and Eamonn Mallie, *The Provisional IRA* (1987). On loyalist paramilitaries see Steve Bruce, *The Red Hand: Protestant Paramilitaries in Northern Ireland* (1992); an earlier picture is given in Sarah Nelson, *Ulster's Uncertain Defenders* (1980). Two key books on British Army tactics are Frank Kitson, *Low Intensity Operations: Subversion, Insurgency and Peacekeeping* (1971) and Mark Urban, *Big Boys' Rules* (1992). A cogent indictment of the role of undercover military operations from a nationalist perspective is given by Raymond Murray, *The SAS in Ireland* (1990). The work of the RUC and the UDR has been analysed in two books by Chris Ryder, *The RUC: A Force under Fire* (1989) and *The Ulster Defence Regiment: an Instrument of Peace?* (1991); see also John Brewer, *Inside the RUC: Routine Policing in a Divided Society* (1991). A critical account of the administration of justice under emergency powers is given in Tony Jennings (ed.), *Justice under Fire: the abuse of civil liberties in Northern Ireland*, 2nd ed. (1992).

References

1. Two official inquiries, the Stalker–Sampson and the Stevens investigations, have been carried out into these allegations. Neither has been released in full; see John Stalker, *Stalker* (1988) and Peter Taylor, *Stalker: The Search for Truth* (1987).

2. See the *Annual Reports of the Chief Constable of the Royal Ulster Constabulary* for 1990 to 1992.

3. See Kevin Boyle, Tom Hadden and Paddy Hillyard, *Ten Years On in Northern Ireland* (1980), Chapter 3, and Louise Shara, 'Thugs and Hooligans', *Fortnight*, Issue 325 (1994).

4. Frank Burton, *The Politics of Legitimacy: Struggles in a Belfast*

Community (1978); Sarah Nelson, *Ulster's Uncertain Defenders* (1980); J. Sluka, *Hearts and Minds, Water and Fish: Support for the IRA and INLA in a Northern Irish Ghetto* (1989).

5. J. Sluka, *Hearts and Minds, Water and Fish: Support for the IRA and INLA in a Northern Irish Ghetto* (1989), Chapter 4.

6. Helsinki Watch, *Children in Northern Ireland* (1992).

7. See John Stalker, *Stalker* (1988); Mark Urban, *Big Boys' Rules* (1992).

8. *Ireland* v *United Kingdom* (1982), 4 EHRR 40.

9. The ending of internment was recommended by the Gardiner Committee, Cmnd. 5847 (1985).

10. Peter Taylor, *Beating the Terrorists?* (1980).

11. The official response to these allegations was the appointment of Sir Louis Blom-Cooper as Independent Commissioner for the Holding Centres on a non-statutory basis.

12. See John Stalker, *Stalker* (1988).

13. Mark Urban, *Big Boys' Rules* (1992).

14. *McEldowney* v *Forde* (1971), A. C. 632.

15. *Report of the Diplock Committee*, Cmnd. 5185 (1972).

16. Kevin Boyle, Tom Hadden and Paddy Hillyard, *Ten Years on in Northern Ireland: the legal control of political violence* (1980), Chapter 6.

17. *Review of the Northern Ireland (Emergency Provisions) Acts* (1990), Cm. 1115.

18. *Brogan* v *United Kingdom* (1989), 11 EHRR 117.

19. See the report of the Widgery Tribunal into the 'Bloody Sunday' shootings in Londonderry on 30 January 1972, 1971–72 H. C. 220; and the report of the Bennett Committee into RUC interrogation procedures (1979), Cmnd. 7497.

20. Commissioners have been appointed on a non-statutory basis to

review the operation of emergency powers and to supervise interrogation centres; and on a statutory basis to monitor complaints against the Army.

21. *Ireland* v *United Kingdom* (1982), 4 EHRR 40.

22. *Brogan* v *United Kingdom* (1989), 11 EHRR 117.

23. *Ireland* v *United Kingdom* (1982), 4 EHRR 40.

24. *McFeely* v *United Kingdom* (1981), 2 EHRR 161.

25. *Stewart* v *United Kingdom* (1985), 7 EHRR 453.

26. *Kelly* v *United Kingdom* (13 January 1993).

27. *Brannigan* v *United Kingdom* (26 May 1993).

28. See, for example, Helsinki Watch, *Human Rights in Northern Ireland* (1991).

CHAPTER 4   **The Peacemakers**

General reading

A good general introduction to the role of religion and the churches in Northern Ireland is given in the Report of the Opsahl Commission, *A Citizens' Inquiry* (1993), Chapters 9 and 10. For a sustained Christian analysis of the Northern Ireland conflict and possible solutions see the Report of an Interchurch Group on Faith and Politics, *Breaking down the Enmity* (1993).

References

1. An example is the long-established work of Protestant and Catholic Encounter (PACE) and of the recently formed inter-faith group, Faith and Politics; for a current analysis see Inge Radford, *Breaking Down Divisions: the possibilities of a local church contribution to improving community relations*, Northern Ireland Community Relations Council (1993).

2. See Ray Davey, *A Channel of Peace: the Story of the Corrymeela Community* (1993).

3. The Churches' Religious Education Core Syllabus Drafting Group, *Religious Education* (1992); Northern Ireland Curriculum Council, *Guidance Materials for Religious Education* (1993).

4. On these issues generally see Chris Moffat (ed.), *Education Together for a Change* (1993).

5. Ed Moloney and Andy Pollak, *Paisley* (1986).

6. Duncan Morrow, *The Churches and Inter-Community Relations* (1991).

7. Bob Purdie, *Politics in the Streets: the Origins of the Civil Rights Movement in Northern Ireland* (1990).

8. Ciaran McKeown, *The Passion of Peace* (1984).

9. The full range of projects is listed in the *Third Annual Report of the Northern Ireland Community Relations Council* (1993).

10. The Council has always used the less exclusive expression 'cultural traditions'; see the reports of a series of Cultural Traditions Group Conferences: *Varieties of Irishness* (1989); *Varieties of Britishness* (1990); *All European Now?* (1991). See also the report of a Co-operation North Conference, *Whose Music?* (1992).

11. The establishment and work of the International Fund is analysed in Tom Hadden and Kevin Boyle, *The Anglo-Irish Agreement* (1989), Chapter 3.

12. A detailed evaluation of the government-funded community relations projects of District Councils reported an increasing acceptance of the importance of community relations by local politicians and some evidence from opinion surveys of an improvement in relations between Protestants and Catholics in some areas: Colin Knox *et al.*, *A Policy Evaluation of the District Council Community Relations Programme* (1993).

13. The impact of District Council schemes in 'hardline areas' was reported to be small; ibid., p. 10.

14. For a detailed account and evaluation of these initiatives see *Ireland: A Positive Proposal* (1985), Chapter 5 and *The Anglo-Irish Agreement* (1989), Chapter 1.

15. *A Citizens' Inquiry: the Opsahl Report on Northern Ireland* (1993).

16. *Fortnight*, Issue 320 (1993).

CHAPTER 5   The European Context

General reading

For a general account of economic issues in Northern Ireland see Richard Harris, Clifford Jefferson and John Spencer, *The Northern Ireland Economy* (1990). For European aspects see the report of a conference organized by the Northern Ireland Centre in Europe, *Network Europe* (1993), and the report of a Norwegian Institute of International Affairs conference, *The Republic of Ireland and Northern Ireland in a European Context* (1993). For an introductory account of the Conference on Security and Cooperation in Europe see University of Essex Human Rights Centre Papers No. 1, Rachel Brett, *The Development of the Human Dimension Mechanism of the CSCE* (1991).

References

1. Bob Rowthorn and N. Wayne, *Northern Ireland: The Political Economy of Conflict* (1988).

2. Vani Borooah, 'Northern Ireland – Portrait of a Regional Economy', in *Network Europe*, p. 108, the report of a conference organized by the Northern Ireland Centre in Europe.

3. Ibid., p. 112.

4. Bob Rowthorn and N. Wayne, *Northern Ireland: The Political Economy of Conflict* (1988).

5. Parliamentary Answer, 6 July 1993.

6. *Regional Trends* 26 (1993), Table 2.1.

7. Northern Ireland Economic Research Centre Survey (1990).

8. See *Network Europe*, Section II, the report of a conference organized by the Northern Ireland Centre in Europe.

9. The procedures under the equivalent United Nations Convention against Torture were used to good effect by the Northern Ireland civil liberties body, the Committee on the Administration of Justice, in respect of allegations of ill-treatment at Castlereagh in 1992.

CHAPTER 6   Structures for Sharing

General reading

For a general discussion of political accommodation in divided societies see Arend Lijphart, *Democracy in Plural Societies* (1977). For some examples of constitutional mechanisms for divided societies see Minority Rights Group Pamphlet No. 36, Claire Palley, *Constitutional Law and Minorities* (1982). For a detailed assessment of possible models for Northern Ireland see John McGarry and Brendan O'Leary, *The Future of Northern Ireland* (1991). For a discussion of relationships between the different peoples of the British Isles see Hugh Kearney, *The British Isles: a History of Four Nations* (1989). For a good discussion of the application of international standards on human rights to Northern Ireland see Liberty, *Broken Covenants* (1993).

References

1. *A Citizens' Inquiry: The Opsahl Report on Northern Ireland* (1993), Chapter 10.

2. See the *Report of the Northern Ireland Constitutional Convention* (1976).

3. Northern Ireland Act 1982, section 2.

4. *Ireland: A Positive Proposal*, Chapter 6.

5. Davy, Kelleher and McCarthy, *Macroeconomic Consequences of Integrated Economic Policy, Planning and Co-ordination in Ireland* (1984).

6. *Northern Ireland: Report of an Independent Inquiry* (1984).

7. Brendan O'Leary *et al.*, *Northern Ireland: Sharing Authority* (1993).

244 Northern Ireland: The Choice

8. *A Citizens' Inquiry: The Opsahl Report on Northern Ireland* (1993), Chapter 10.

9. Standing Advisory Commission on Human Rights, *Second Report on Religious and Political Discrimination and Equality of Opportunity in Northern Ireland* (1990), Cm. 1107, para 8.41.

10. See generally the forthcoming report on the democratic deficit in Northern Ireland prepared for the Democratic Audit of the United Kingdom by John Morison and Stephen Livingstone.

11. *Review Body on Local Government in Northern Ireland* (1970), Cmd. 546.

12. The issues in this paragraph are discussed in C. Moffat (ed.), *Education Together for a Change* (1993), Introduction.

13. David Smith and Gerry Chambers, *Equality and Inequality in Northern Ireland 4: Public Housing*, Policy Studies Institute Occasional Paper 47 (1988), pp. 57–8.

14. Northern Ireland Housing Executive Research Unit, *Public Attitudes Survey* (1990), Figure 7.

15. Standing Advisory Commission on Human Rights, *Second Report on Religious and Political Discrimination and Equality of Opportunity in Northern Ireland* (1990), Cm. 1107, paras. 4.53–54 and 6.19.

16. *A Citizens' Inquiry: The Opsahl Report on Northern Ireland* (1993), Chapter 10.

17. Standing Advisory Commission on Human Rights, *The Protection of Human Rights by Law in Northern Ireland* (1977), Cmnd. 7009.

18. The European Court of Human Rights retains the competence to determine whether resort to emergency powers is justified, but grants a wide margin of appreciation to individual governments.

19. Minority Rights Group Pamphlet No. 36, Claire Palley, *Constitutional Law and Minorities* (1982).

20. Standing Advisory Commission on Human Rights, *Second Report on Religious and Political Discrimination and Equality of Opportunity in Northern Ireland* (1990), Cm. 1107, paras. 4.18 ff.

21. Ibid., para. 8.41.

22. This approach is recommended in the IPPR Report, para 4.20; see note 7 above.

23. A survey of the wide range of cross-border economic and social cooperation was published after the meeting of the Anglo-Irish Ministerial Conference on 11 March 1986; see Tom Hadden and Kevin Boyle, *The Anglo-Irish Agreement* (1989), pp. 43–5.

24. The Northern Ireland legislation is the Foyle Fisheries Act (Northern Ireland) 1952; the Irish legislation is the Foyle Fisheries Act 1952. The wording of both laws is often identical.

25. In a recent test case raised by unionists Articles 2 and 3 were held by the Irish Supreme Court to make the pursuit of Irish unification a 'constitutional imperative', *McGimpsey* v *Ireland* (1992), Irish Reports 110.

26. See Kevin Boyle, 'The Irish Question and Human Rights in European Perspectives', in H. O. Skar and B. Lydersen (eds.), *Northern Ireland: A Critical Test for a Europe of Peaceful Regions* (1993), and John A. Murphy, 'Ireland: Identity and Relationships', in Bernard Crick (ed.), *National Identities: The Constitution of the United Kingdom* (1991).

27. See G. P. Nielsson, 'The parallel national action process: Scandinavian experiences', in P. Taylor and A. J. R. Groom (eds.), *International Organisation: A Conceptual Approach* (1978).

CHAPTER 7   **Structures for Separation**

General reading

For a comparative analysis of models for dealing with ethnic divisions see John McGarry and Brendan O'Leary, *The Politics of Ethnic Conflict Regulation* (1993); on repartition see Liam Kennedy, 'Repartition' in John McGarry and Brendan O'Leary (eds.) *The Future of Northern Ireland* (1990).

References

1. Romansh is the least secure of these and has no firm cultural basis. The official languages are German, French and Italian.

2. For an up-to-date account of recent constitutional developments see André Alen (ed.), *Treatise on Belgian Constitutional Law* (1992).

3. For a translation of the constitutional provisions cited see J. G. and G. J. Craenen, *The Constitution of the Kingdom of Belgium* (1991).

4. *Case relating to certain aspects of the laws on the use of languages in Belgium* (1968) Series A, No. 6; see also *Mathieu-Mohin and Clerfayt v Belgium* (1987), Series A, No. 113.

5. For a discussion of the operation and merits of this exemption see Standing Advisory Commission on Human Rights, *Report on Fair Employment* (1987), Cm. 237, paras. 8.24–8.39.

6. There is already a convention that some representatives of both communities in Northern Ireland are appointed to the Irish Senate. There is also a growing movement to extend the Irish franchise to Irish people living abroad.

CHAPTER 8   **Getting There**

General reading

The various dimensions of the right to self-determination are discussed in James Crawford (ed.), *The Rights of Peoples* (1988) and Hurst Hannum, *Autonomy, Sovereignty and Self-Determination: the accommodation of conflicting rights* (1990).

References

1. *A Citizens' Inquiry: The Opsahl Report on Northern Ireland* (1993), p. 68.

2. See the *Report of the Special Rapporteur on the Historical and Current Developments of the Right to Self-Determination* (Critescu Report) (1980), UN Doc E/CN.4/Sub.2/404/Rev. 1.

3. See generally Minority Rights Group Pamphlet No. 2, Harold Jackson and Anne McHardy, *Two Irelands: The Problem of the Double Minority* (3rd ed.) (1984).

4. Ibid., p. 35.

5. A weighted majority vote of 75 per cent of those voting in a referendum has been recommended in the IPPR Report by Brendan O'Leary *et al.*, *Northern Ireland: Sharing Authority*, p. 44.

6. Arend Lijphart, *Democracy in Plural Societies* (1977).

7. Brendan O'Leary *et al.*, *Northern Ireland: Sharing Authority* (1993), p. 146.

8. See generally Frederick Rowe, *A History of Newfoundland and Labrador* (1980).

9. The negotiations leading to the referendums are recorded in detail in *Documents on Relations between Canada and Newfoundland, Vol. 2, 1940–49* (1984).

10. For a discussion of the preferendum concept see Peter Emerson, 'Preferred Alternative', *Fortnight*, Issue 313 (1993).

11. See University of Essex Human Rights Centre Papers No. 2, Rachel Brett, *The Challenges of Change: Report of the Helsinki Follow-up Meeting of the CSCE* (1992).

Index

Leipzig, 115
lethal force, 99, 101
Liberal Democrats, 58
Libya, 88
Lijphart, Arend, 217–18, 220, 243, 247
Livingstone, Stephen, 244
local government, 14, 173–5
London, 74, 107
London/Derry
    City, 5, 6, 11, 83–4, 194, 205
    County, 24
loyalist
    definition, 22
    terrorism, 74–5, 78–80

Maastricht Treaty, 143, 145–7, 168, 232
McBride Principles, 219
McCrea, William, 112
Macrory Report, 174
McEldowney v Forde, 239
McFeely v United Kingdom, 240
McGarry, John, 243, 245
McGimpsey v Ireland, 245
McHardy, Anne, 247
McKeown, Ciaran, 241
Magherafelt, 26, 74
Maguire, Mairead, 114
Major, John, xiii, 131
Malaya, 84
Mallie, Eamonn, 238
Manila, 115
Markets, 5
Maryfield, 121
Masonic Order, 39
Mater Hospital, 196
Methodist Church, 110
minorities, 17, 135–6
mixed marriage, 23, 28, 65, 111
Moffat, Chris, 235, 241, 244
Moloney, Ed, 241
Molyneaux, Jim, 57
Monaghan, County, 24, 30
Morison, John, 244
Morrow, Duncan, 241
Motorman, Operation, 11, 86
Mourne Mountains, 24, 34
Moyle, 26, 205
Moxon-Browne, Eddie, 237
multinationals, 136
Murphy, John, 245

Murray, Raymond, 235, 238

nationalist
    definition, 22
    voting, 55
Nelson, Sarah, 238, 239
Netherlands
    'grand compromise', 158, 163
    Oost Region, 141
    sharing in, 17
Newfoundland, 221–3
New Ireland Forum, 127, 140, 155, 165–6, 169
New Lodge, 81
Nielsson, G.P., 245
Nordic Council, 191
no-go areas, 11, 86
North England, 30, 50–51
Northern Ireland
    Act 1974, 223
    Assembly, 55, 123, 162–3, 167, 168, 184, 221
    Bill of Rights, 180–86
    border poll, 59
    British subvention, 137, 139–40, 165–6
    Constitution, 161, 179, 181–6, 211, 214, 224, 230
    Constitutional Convention, 120, 140, 223
    cooperation with Republic, 13, 186–90
    Council for Integrated Education, 195
    district councils, 14
    Economic Research Centre, 242
    economy, 137–42
    (Emergency Provisions) Acts, 95–6
    Housing Executive, 35, 38, 177, 236, 244
    Labour Party, 58
    relative prosperity, 140–41
    trade, 141–2
North–South relations, 186–90
Norway, 191
Norwegian Institute, 242

O'Brien, Brendan, 238
O Fiacch, Tomas, 112
Official IRA, 76
Official Unionist Party, *see* Ulster Unionist Party